Abortion in the United States

This book explores the seismic shift brought about by the 2022 US Supreme Court decision in *Dobbs v. Jackson Women's Health Organization*, which dramatically changed the constitutional standing of abortion decisions set in place by *Roe v. Wade* 50 years earlier. The authors describe the history of US Supreme Court's decision-making around abortion and some of its attendant considerations, including the constitutional right to privacy, moral obligations to protect life, and determinations about when life begins.

When Dobbs was decided, legal control over abortion was returned to the states, resulting in wildly divergent access to abortion across the nation. As important, Dobbs raised a host of additional legal and moral questions that will no doubt be the focus of many future courtroom and legislative debates.

This text is designed for undergraduate students across a range of academic disciplines. It lays bare the complicated moral dimensions of the competing arguments about abortion and how these considerations have fared in legal decisions, so students can make sense of them for themselves.

Elyshia Aseltine is an associate professor at Towson University (TU) in Maryland. Her research focuses on racial inequalities and the criminal justice system. She is also the College of Liberal Arts Mitten Professor, the founding director of TU's Fair Chance Higher Education initiative, and a 2019 Open Society Institute-Baltimore Community Fellow.

Sheldon Ekland-Olson is Rapoport Professor and Provost Emeritus at the University of Texas, Austin. He taught in the Department of Sociology, Law School, and Honors Programs. He was dean of the College of Liberal Arts for five years and Executive Vice President and Provost for eight years. He is the recipient of numerous university-wide and system-wide teaching awards. He is currently retired.

Abortion in the United States

The Moral and Legal Landscape

Elyshia Aseltine and Sheldon Ekland-Olson

Routledge
Taylor & Francis Group

NEW YORK AND LONDON

First published 2025
by Routledge
605 Third Avenue, New York, NY 10158

and by Routledge
4 Park Square, Milton Park, Abingdon, Oxon, OX14 4RN

Routledge is an imprint of the Taylor & Francis Group, an informa business

© 2025 Elyshia Aseltine and Sheldon Ekland-Olson

ISBN: 978-1-032-55423-5 (hbk)
ISBN: 978-1-032-55422-8 (pbk)
ISBN: 978-1-003-43060-5 (ebk)

DOI: 10.4324/9781003430605

Typeset in Times New Roman
by Apex CoVantage, LLC

Contents

1 Abortion's Shifting Landscape

Introduction

In a stark, though anticipated, decision released on June 24, 2022, the Supreme Court of the United States decided they had been wrong. In *Dobbs v. Jackson Women's Health Organization,* the Court held (6–3), contravening almost 50 years of prior Supreme Court decisions, that the choice to have an abortion was not a constitutional right of a woman but an action that could be regulated by state legislatures.

The *Dobbs* decision, like the *Roe v. Wade* decision it overturned, changed the national landscape of abortion. Its effect was dramatic and immediate. What had been settled law became an open question with wide-ranging implications. Anticipating the *Dobbs* decision, many states had laws waiting in the wings. What follows explores this background and shifting landscape.

A General Framework: Dealing With Life-Threatening Dilemmas

Shifting abortion practices, legislation, and court findings will occupy the bulk of our attention, but first we take a brief look at a general framework. Specifically, it is important to recognize life is infused with dilemmas, some driven by moral considerations, some not. The nature of moral dilemmas is that whichever decision is made, the contending alternative becomes problematic. Tension cannot be avoided. Abortion decisions are filled with such moral dilemmas. Who should decide: the individuals most immediately involved, the legislature, the courts? What factors should be taken into consideration?

Empathy and assessments of social worth organize and guide how we deal with this dilemma-driven tension. **The Trolley Problem**, which has been presented in numerous forms, illustrates:

A trolley is coming down the track. Some 300 yards ahead, five men are tied to the track. They will surely die unless something is done. You notice there is a lever within your reach. If you pull it, you can redirect the train to another

DOI: 10.4324/9781003430605-1

track and save the five men. Easy, you will simply pull the lever. Easy until you notice there is another man tied to the sidetrack. Will you pull the lever, or not?

When this dilemma has been presented to audiences, between 75% and 80% of respondents say they would pull the lever. They don't feel good about it, but they would save five lives for the price of one. Among those who would not pull the lever, various reasons are given. Many draw the distinction between killing someone and letting someone die. They don't want to act to kill the single man, even if it means letting the others die. They, too, are uneasy with their choice.

Decisions change when empathy-laced variations are presented. What would you do if the lone person is your close friend and the five are unknown strangers? What about five derelicts and your young child? Examples abound, up to and including torturing individuals to save others or going to war to kill "them" and save "us."

Similarly, empathy holds a central place when we consider the fetus as a clump of cells as opposed to an unborn child. Alternatively, do we ignore the suffering of a young woman who became pregnant by reason of rape or incestual abuse in favor of the child yet to be born? Moral dilemmas are resolved in part by setting priorities, adjusted according to variation in perceived social worth and the resulting levels of empathy. Whatever the choice, by the dilemma's very nature, tension remains.

When does abortion become infanticide? Should life-protecting measures be taken at the moment of conception (perhaps before)? Are there empathetic shifts when signs of life, perhaps a heartbeat or the fetal ability to experience suffering, become observable? Is it when the developing fetus resembles a human in appearance? Is it when the newborn takes its first breath? Much depends on empathy.

Then there are other considerations. What about the suffering of the mother? Should a rape-induced pregnancy be treated the same as a pregnancy resulting from loving sexual intercourse? Does the age of a 14-year-old child who is pregnant due to the abuse of her uncle make a difference? What about the comparison of the choices involved? A couple wants to have a child using *in vitro* fertilization (IVF), knowing that in the process numerous fertilized eggs may be discarded. If life begins at conception, should IVF be legal? If the choice must be made between the life of the mother and the not-yet-born infant, what choice should be allowed? What about an abortion when a serious defect in the fetus is discovered? How serious of a defect? The questions are many. They are intertwined. These are the questions before us.

An Overview of Abortion in the United States

The story begins with the idea that protections should be given to the *possibility* of any human life. Within this framework, protected life begins prior to conception. The idea is that we should not tamper with the process of creating life. This was the position taken by the Catholic Church when considering the use of contraception.

Laws grounded in such moral and religious beliefs restrict access to, and use of, contraception. Such laws were once widespread in the United States. When implemented, they came to be known as Comstock Laws to recognize the drafter of early federal legislation. We will see how these laws were eventually challenged on several fronts, most energetically when "the pill" to regulate conception became widely available.

Legal change came when two contraception cases were decided by the US Supreme Court, one from Connecticut and one from Massachusetts. These cases were linked and grounded in the Supreme Court's holding that there was a constitutional right to privacy. Making the highly personal choice to use contraceptives was one such choice. Protected life, the Supreme Court held, did not begin prior to conception. There was a right to decide, as the Court put it, "whether or not to bear or beget a child." The use of contraceptives was a private, constitutionally protected decision. These two cases set the foundation for *Roe v. Wade*.

With the choice to use contraception legally protected, attention turned to balancing the mother's and fetus's lives and implications of the mother's choices during gestation. Two dramatic events, one in Arizona and one in California, set the stage and informed the eventual *Roe v. Wade* decision. With *Roe,* the fetus, once viable, took on the attributes of protected personhood. The protected life of the viable fetus was balanced against the mother's life, health, and choices she might make. Absent viability, the Court argued, women should have the right to choose. The *Roe* case, like the subsequent Dobbs decision, produced a seismic shift. After the decisions, what was formerly illegal became legal. *Roe* was decided in 1973. Political pressure, subsequent court cases, and violence followed. These will be explored in more detail.

For many of those opposed to *Roe,* the question became: Should they obey God's will or follow the law? Strategies for restricting women's ability to obtain a now-legal abortion were crafted. In addition to political turmoil, there were several subsequent Supreme Court cases. In 1992, one such case, *Planned Parenthood of Southeastern Pennsylvania v. Casey*, was decided. In *Casey,* the court considered restrictions a state may place on a person seeking an abortion. If such restrictions imposed an "undue burden," they were unconstitutional. Subsequent developments in practices, policies, and law followed and will be reviewed.

Roe and *Casey*, along with a handful of additional cases, defined the abortion terrain until 2022, when *Dobbs* was released and overruled these cases. Central to the Supreme Court's findings was the constitutional standing of privacy. With *Dobbs*, the Supreme Court held, "The Constitution does not confer a right to abortion; Roe and Casey are overruled; and the authority to regulate abortion is returned to the people and their elected representatives." With *Dobbs,* the constitutional boundaries of protected life and privacy, as an element of constitutionally protected freedom, again shifted, and legal control over abortion returned to the States.

We will see how, in anticipation of this reversal, many states passed restrictive abortion statutes, with various gestation times after which abortion would be prohibited. In some instances, exceptions were granted or prohibited for incest and rape. In addition, various prohibitive state statutes outlined punishments for those who provided or otherwise assisted in abortions. Other states continued to allow abortions, following the *Roe* and *Casey* guidelines. Adjusting to the new environment, mobile abortion units appeared on state borders, prohibiting and permitting states to address the continued demand.

The *Dobbs* decision brought into question the constitutional standing of gestating life and the significance of privacy when making decisions. If privacy is no longer constitutionally protected, this has far-reaching implications. If states prohibit abortion at conception, what implications are there for use of the "morning after" pill? What about other postconception contraceptives? What is the legal standing of IVF methods of conceiving children when we know unused conceptuses may be discarded? Is there no longer a right to privacy? What are the implications for same-sex marriage? What about interracial marriages? Can restrictive states prosecute those who receive abortions in a less restrictive neighboring State? What about those who assist abortion seekers in various ways? The list goes on. The closing sections will address these questions.

Abortion-related US Supreme Court Decisions

Case	Year	Decision Summary
Roe v. Wade	1973	The fundamental "right to privacy" protects a pregnant woman's choice whether to have an abortion for any reason during the first trimester of pregnancy. A state may regulate abortion in the second and third trimesters so long as the laws contain exceptions protecting the life or health of the mother.
Webster v. Reproductive Health Services	1989	The state can restrict the use of state resources for abortion-related services.
Planned Parenthood of Southeastern Pennsylvania v. Casey	1992	State efforts to regulate abortion prior to viability cannot impose an "undue burden."
Stenberg v. Carhart	2000	Abortion bans needed to include exceptions to preserve a woman's health, and choices about which medical procedure to utilize should be left to appropriate medical judgment.
Gonzales v. Carhart	2007	Bans on specific medically supported abortion procedures must include a health exception.
Whole Woman's Health v. Hellerstedt	2016	States cannot place substantial obstacles (i.e., undue burdens) in the path of women seeking an abortion.
Dobbs v. Jackson Women's Health Organization	2022	The right to an abortion is not implicitly protected by any constitutional provision, and the regulation of abortion should be left up to the states.

Public Opinion

The *Dobbs* decision was released on June 24, 2022. *The New York Times* and The Pew Research Center, in May and early June of that year, reviewed related findings from public opinion polls.[1] At the time, roughly six-in-ten Americans felt abortion should be legal in all or most cases. Evidence from all manner of polls, however, indicated the country's stance on abortion was regionally splintered.

Support was highest in the far West, as well as sections of the northern Midwest and the Northeast. Topping the charts were residents of Vermont, Massachusetts, and Washington, D.C. at 70%. Those opposed were found in what is loosely referred to as the Bible Belt in the southern tier of states, in this case citizens of Louisiana, Arkansas, and Mississippi (36%, 38%, and 39% supported abortion in these states, respectively). Highly educated respondents were more likely to support legal abortion than those with a high school education or less (69% versus 54%), and females were more supportive than males (63% versus 58%). Finally, Catholics (56%) are more supportive than evangelical Protestants (24%).

Measuring Public Opinion on Abortion

Though positions on abortion are often reported as a binary, since at least the 1970s, polls have consistently demonstrated that most Americans hold a "middle position" and support abortion under at least some circumstances. Varying considerations, such as stage of pregnancy, whether the pregnancy endangers a woman's life, whether a baby has severe birth defects, the age of the woman, and the circumstances of the pregnancy (e.g., rape, incest), change respondents answers about their support of abortion.[2]

Though few public opinion surveys ask about possible consequences for those who participate in an illegal abortion, these responses also show great variability. Respondents are most punitive with providers of illegal abortions, but even then, just one in four people would support jail time for such providers. Half of respondents believe that women who obtain an illegal abortion should not be penalized; similarly, more than half feel that those who assist in an illegal abortion (i.e., paying for, finding, or scheduling) should not be penalized.[3]

Patterns in Use

For much of the 1970s and 1980s, over 1.5 million abortions were performed annually in the United States. After 30 years of decline, there is evidence of a recent upswing in the number of abortions. In 2020, there were over 930,000 abortions performed in the United States; approximately one in five pregnancies ended in abortion. Abortions were obtained by women in all US states, though there is wide regional variation: in 2020, 25% of all abortions were obtained in the Northeast, 16% in the Midwest, 34% in the South, and 25% in the West.[4]

How this recent increase is linked to the availability of "the morning after" pill and other medications such as Misoprostol and Mifepristone, approved by the Food and Drug Administration (FDA) (in 1999 and 2000, respectively) to end early pregnancies (up to ten weeks of gestation), is unclear. Whatever the role played by these medications, there was evidence that they were safe and effective and that by 2020, slightly more than half the abortions in the United States relied on these medications.[5]

What are the backgrounds of women who chose abortion? What were their life circumstances and experiences? Some general findings from 2014[6]:

- The majority were in their twenties and thirties (60% and 25%, respectively).
- Most were white (39%), black (28%), or Hispanic (25%). Some were Asian/Pacific Islander (6%) or another race/ethnicity (3%).
- Approximately 75% were low-income.
- Forty-five percent were married or cohabitating—the remainder were never married (46%) or previously married (9%).
- Most (62%) reported a religious affiliation, with Catholic being the most common (24%).
- Close to 60% had given birth at least once before.
- Most paid out of pocket for their procedure (53%).

Finally, why do women choose to have an abortion?[7] Reasons vary, and often women have multiple reasons. The most common reasons are financial (e.g., unable to afford a child), timing (e.g., having a child would interfere with a woman's education, career, or other responsibilities), partner-related (e.g., not wanting to be a single parent, having relationship problems), and other child-related (e.g., the need to focus on other children, having completed their childbearing). For a smaller subset of women, abortion was sought because of maternal or fetal health concerns.

A Brief History of Controlling Childbearing

Women have long tried to control their childbearing.[8] Archaeological evidence of women using contraceptive devices and abortion techniques has been found in Egyptian papyrus dating as early as 1550 BC. These records describe ineffective strategies such as wiping out the vagina after intercourse, as well as Egyptians use of honey, pepper, alum, and lactic acid as contraceptive barriers. Silphion, an herb used in and exported by Greece as an oral abortifacient, was harvested to extinction, and relief sculptures from 1150 AD depict massage abortions in Asian cultures.

Despite rapid changes in communication, scientific knowledge, and public health brought about by the Industrial Revolution in the 19th century, efforts to control childbearing remained largely unscientific and unspoken, in part because of increasingly hostile attitudes toward sex and contraception. Yet, women in the United States were having fewer children—in 1800 women had an average of seven children; by 1900, the average was four. While some of these reductions were likely due to reduced sexual intercourse, other forms of intercourse (anal and oral), and the use of spermicides and condoms, abortion played "an important role."[9] The most common methods of abortion were tonics or pills (including poisons or substances we now know cause cancer) and the injection of fluids or insertion of objects into the uterus. Abortions through dilation and vacuum aspiration were used as early as 1863. Finally, though the scientific knowledge necessary for the creation of birth control pills existed in the 1930s, the costs of mass producing such pills were prohibitive until the 1950s. The first birth control pill was approved by the US Federal and Drug Administration in 1960.[10]

With this background and these experiences in mind, how did we arrive at the *Dobbs* decision?

Establishing the Constitutional Right to Privacy

Establishing the constitutional right to privacy was a major first step. The questions addressed were: Was there a constitutionally protected right to privacy? If so, did this right protect the choice to use contraceptives?

Contraceptives are now widely used and highly effective. Today, many would think prohibiting their use would be nonsensical. Yet, many such laws were once on the books. How were such laws justified? The idea was anchored in the teachings of the Catholic Church, as reaffirmed by Pope Paul VI in 1968, who wrote:

Each and every marital act must of necessity retain its intrinsic relationship to the procreation of human life. . . . We are obliged once more to declare that the direct interruption of the generative process already begun . . . (is) to be absolutely excluded as lawful means of regulating the number of children . . . excluded is any action which either before, at the moment of, or after sexual intercourse, is specifically intended to prevent procreation whether as an end or as a means.[11]

For the Pope, LIFE writ large was sacred and should be protected. Protected life began prior to conception. Contraception was against God's plan. From this doctrine, many anti-contraception laws were crafted and passed.

The Catholic Church and Contraception

The Catholic Church has been instrumental in shaping the national debate around contraception and abortion, often advocating for the strictest limitations on any control of childbearing. One scholar contends, "The Catholic church, which in many human affairs now has the beautiful voice of a skylark, still hangs over decisions related to fertility with the claws of an eagle."[12] Despite the influence of the church, however, there is good reason to believe that the views of its membership and of at least some of its lower-ranking leaders are far more fractured.

As early as the 1930s, the Vatican, "in a contrived and convoluted way," approved the use of the rhythm method (i.e., timing intercourse to reduce or increase the likelihood of pregnancy) for family planning. In the early 1960s, John Rock, co-inventor of the Pill and pioneer of IVF, was a regular advocate of birth control on American television and print news. He was also a devout Catholic and author of "The Time Has Come: A Catholic Doctor's Proposals to End the Battle Over Birth Control."[13] In 1962, the Vatican Council agreed that the primary aim of marriage is mutual love rather than procreation; in addition, "practically all theologians of stature began to develop an ethical system that embraced so-called artificial contraception." The support for these ideas within the church was gaining such momentum that, in 1963, Pope Paul IV set up a special commission to reexamine the church's position on contraception. A majority (9 of the 16) of bishops in the group voted to allow for the use of artificial contraception. To the surprise of many, when the Pope finally issued the encyclical Humanae Vitae, he upheld, rather than relaxed, the church's ban on birth control. His decision rippled throughout the church, resulting in theologians being dismissed as well as priests and parishioners alike leaving the church. In the United States, the percentage of Catholics who attended weekly mass dropped from 71% to 50%.[14]

By the 1970s, fertility rates for US Catholics converged with those of other faiths (about two children), a trend that continues today.[15] And Catholic women are as likely to get an abortion as other women[16] and more likely to get an abortion than women from other religious groups.[17]

Numerous events and scientific developments in the mid-20th century raised challenges to decades-old anti-contraception laws. Broad-based modification of the law was provided some three years prior to Pope Paul VI's encyclical when, in 1965, the US Supreme Court, voting 7-2, found a right to privacy in the "penumbras" of the Constitution.

Specifically, the Court found that "A right to privacy can be inferred from several amendments in the Bill of Rights, and this right prevents states from making the use of contraception by married couples illegal." The case, *Griswold v. Connecticut,*[18] struck down Connecticut's state law, which had been on the books since 1879, just short of a century.

Connecticut's law was patterned after the 1873 federal law authored by a New Yorker, Anthony Comstock. In addition to Catholic doctrine, the federal law was born from a concern with obscenity, the belief being that publicizing, distributing, and using contraceptives would encourage immoral behavior. Along with Connecticut's statute, 23 similar "Comstock" laws in other states were crafted shortly after 1873. Connecticut's law was among the most restrictive, where even married couples could be arrested for using birth control and subjected to a one-year prison sentence. While the law was rarely enforced, it had remained on the books for some 90 years.

Comstock Laws

Anthony Comstock, former dry goods salesman turned United States Postal Inspector and founder of the New York Society for the Suppression of Vice, was very concerned about sexual morality in the late 19th century. Contraception and abortion caused him particular ire, as he believed that they directly contributed to vices such as prostitution, pre/extramarital sex, and illegitimacy.

By 1873, Comstock had successfully lobbied Congress for the passage of the Act for the Suppression of Trade in and Circulation of Obscene Literature and Articles for Immoral Use. Those convicted of violating the act could face jail time, hard labor, and fines up to $2,000. Using the authority of his position as postal inspector, Comstock regularly arrested individuals for mailing "obscene" materials.[19]

In addition to sustained attempts to disrupt the work of birth control advocate Margaret Sanger, Comstock sought to shut down the lucrative business of English immigrant Ann Lohman (alias Madame Restell). At the height of her nearly 40-year run, Lohman operated clinics that offered medicine and surgical abortions in New York, Boston, and Philadelphia. Lohman spent as much as $60,000 a year advertising her services for "indisposed women" in medical journals and newspapers. Lohman was arrested several times, the last time by Comstock in the mid-1970s. The night before her trial, Lohman died by suicide. She died a millionaire.[20]

Contraceptives were confiscated by US postal service until 1937, when a ruling of the New York Court of Appeals (*the United States v. One Package*) concluded that Comstock Laws were not intended to prevent materials recommended by physicians for the life and well-being of patients.[21]

Major pressure for change came from the efforts of Margaret Sanger and her fellow activists. In 1916, they had opened a birth control clinic in a low-income neighborhood of Brooklyn, New York. It was a time when eugenics was reaching its height. Eugenics was a social and political movement aimed at limiting the number of "unfit" members of society, a determination infused with biases based on class, race, and ethnicity. How the efforts of Sanger and her colleagues were motivated by their support for eugenics is debated. Clearer was Sangers' motivation to maximize the ability of women to regulate the size of their families.

Sanger, Birth Control, and Eugenics

Margaret Sanger, an Irish-Catholic public health nurse, first became interested in birth control in 1912 after twice caring for a mother of three who had self-administered two abortions. Three months after nursing her patient back from near death after her first abortion, Sanger returned for a visit only to discover the patient had died from injuries sustained because of a second self-induced abortion.[22]

In addition to opening a birth control clinic in New York City, Sanger published magazines and pamphlets on contraceptives, suppositories, and douching. Her efforts around birth control advocacy led directly to the founding of what would eventually become known as the Planned Parenthood Federation of America. Many regard Sanger as the "main force behind the American birth control movement."[23]

While Sanger was critical in reframing the debate around birth control as a private decision rather than a public (and moral) concern, her involvement in the birth control movement is complicated by her participation in the American eugenics movement.

Eugenics is a pseudo-scientific movement grounded in the belief that undesirable social traits are hereditary. Eugenicists advocated for the passage of laws aimed at removing undesirable traits from the "racial stock" through institutionalization in asylums, refusal of marriage licenses, and even permanent sterilization of "defective" individuals. In 1930, 33 states had mandatory sterilization laws on the books.

After becoming disillusioned by the socialist movement (which had little interest in women's issues) and the feminist movement (which had little interest in birth control), Sanger tried to persuade eugenicists to take up the birth control cause. She began including works from prominent eugenicists in her publications and trying to get birth control on the agenda of eugenics conferences. Sanger argued that many of the nation's social problems were the result of overbreeding amongst the working class. If women had more control over their childbearing, they could protect their existing children from moral defect and racial decline, ultimately leading to a "cleaner race." For Sanger, birth control was the "pivot of civilization."[24] Though Sanger's efforts to pull eugenicists into the birth control cause were largely unsuccessful, some use her historical involvement with eugenics to criticize Planned Parenthood and its contemporary reproductive services.[25]

Driven by a sense of injustice, anchored in the repression of women, especially those with few economic means, their pro-contraception efforts following the Great Depression resulted in the founding of what became The Planned Parenthood Federation of America. In fighting for women's right to limit the size of their families, Sanger and her colleagues protested, even to the point of going to jail. For these crusaders, the case was clear. Women should be free to privately plan and determine the size of their families, unencumbered by governmental prohibitions.

As the Great Depression unfolded, economic pressure increased on families to limit their size, and a commitment to challenge the Comstock Laws strengthened. As the demand for contraception grew, science and pharmaceutical companies responded. In 1960, the federal FDA approved Enovid, "the Pill," for birth control.

Enovid, along with other alternatives developed at roughly the same time, dramatically improved both the convenience and effectiveness of birth control options. Demand continued to grow. With the marketplace activated, challenges to limit state intervention increased. Eventually, these challenges found their way to the US Supreme Court.

The specific case involved the head of Planned Parenthood of Connecticut and a colleague doctor, both working with a local birth control clinic. Estelle Griswold, head of Planned Parenthood in Connecticut, was a colleague of C. Lee Buxton, a gynecologist at the Yale School of Medicine. In 1961, they opened a birth control clinic in New Haven. The same day the clinic opened, it received ten patients and dozens of requests from married women who wanted birth control advice and prescriptions.

Shortly thereafter, police officers arrived. Griswold and Buxton were arrested, in a one-day trial, found guilty, and fined $100 each. During the trial, it came out that one clinic patient had nearly died after her last pregnancy and continued to suffer from partial paralysis and impaired speech. Another woman had given birth to three mentally challenged children, each of whom died shortly after birth. Dr. Buxton recommended contraception for both women, believing that another pregnancy could be fatal for the first and seriously unhealthy for the second. The convictions of Griswold and Buxton were upheld by the Appellate Division of the Circuit Court and by Connecticut's Supreme Court. Their case eventually moved to the US Supreme Court.

As noted, the final Supreme Court vote was 7-2, declaring Connecticut's law unconstitutional, but all nine of the Supreme Court Justices, even the two writing in dissent, saw problems. Justice Stewart, one of the two dissenting Justices, used the words "uncommonly silly" and "asinine" to describe Connecticut's law (he, too, thought it should be a personal choice), but disagreed that the law was unconstitutional—nowhere in the Constitution was there a reference to "privacy," "family planning," or "birth control."

In what sense, then, did the Connecticut law violate the US Constitution? Where to look? What to do? Justice Douglas, along with six concurring members of the Court's majority, turned to the implications of the Constitution's general principles. Referring to these principles, Douglas wrote that they "have penumbras, formed by emanations from those guarantees that help give them life and substance."

The final decision of the Court was eventually anchored in the First, Fourth, Fifth, Ninth, and Fourteenth Amendments. Tying these Amendments together, the Justices asserted, was the right to privacy. The Court famously found, "The First Amendment has a penumbra where privacy is protected from governmental intrusion. While it is not expressly included in the First Amendment, its existence is necessary in making the express guarantees fully meaningful." With privacy now anchored in the Constitution, it was a small step to see the use of contraceptives as a matter of private choice. Married couples should be able to exercise that right free of governmental intrusion when it came to the purchase and use of contraceptives. The Connecticut law was unconstitutional.

Seven years later, in 1972, just one court session prior to the release of *Roe v. Wade* in 1973, the protected right to privacy was extended to unmarried persons as well. In this case, William Baird, who had been jailed some eight times for his activist behavior, was lecturing at Boston University on birth control and overpopulation. Following his lecture, he gave Emko Vaginal Foam to a woman who approached him for help. He was charged with and convicted of breaking the Massachusetts Comstock law.

Baird appealed his conviction and sentence. Eventually, he won. The Supreme Court found in *Eisenstadt v. Baird* that

> [i]f under Griswold the distribution of contraceptives to married persons cannot be prohibited, a ban on the distribution to unmarried persons would be equally impermissible, since the constitutionally protected right to privacy inheres in the individual, not the marital couple.

The issue was settled. There was a constitutional right to privacy, and it applied to the regulation of contraceptives used and purchased by married and unmarried persons alike. In their next session, the Court turned to abortion. The question became, when do the boundaries of life become protected?

Thalidomide, Rubella, and Abortion

The science and related technologies producing new pharmaceuticals were not the only advances being made. There were also advances enabling more informed observation and understanding of fetal intrauterine development. By the late 1950s and early 1960s, ultrasound monitoring of the fetus had become widely available. In addition to advances in science and technology, the National Organization for Women (NOW) was officially established on June 30, 1966, and a broad-based movement to improve the standing of women in society was well underway.

Justices on the Supreme Court were aware of the evolving social terrain as well as technologies and pharmaceuticals being developed. These revolutionary changes were joined by two separate events that crystallized thinking across the nation when it came to legalizing abortion. In 1962, the first of these events took shape in the life of Sherri Finkbine, the host of a popular children's TV show, Romper Room. Sherri and her husband, Bob, had four children, all younger than seven years. She had become pregnant with their fifth child. To help with morning sickness, Sherri had been taking a newly developed sedative her husband, a local high school teacher who had chaperoned a group of students on a 1961 European tour, had brought home. The medication turned out to be a high dose of thalidomide. Sherri soon became aware that the dose of thalidomide she was taking was frequently associated with serious, crippling birth defects. She went to her doctor to seek advice. While talking through options, she would later recall him saying, "Sherri, if you were my own wife and we two had four small children, and you really wanted a fifth child, I'd say start again next month under better odds."[26]

Sherri and Bob had a difficult decision to make. They wanted this new child but were confronted by the high probability it would be born with serious birth defects and have a short life. Sherri would later recall:

> It's ironic that someone as child oriented as I am would become known as an abortion advocate, or precipitate what would become the divisive Pro Life/ Pro Choice movement. Perhaps it helps to quell the idiotic suggestions that only women who hate children or men, want to end pregnancies.[27]

Early-term abortions were available in Arizona, though only through a walking-on-the-edge interpretation of an Arizona law. Sherri decided to avoid the local Catholic medical center but contacted another hospital to set an abortion appointment for the following Monday. Sherri also wanted to send cautionary words about thalidomide to other mothers and families, especially as she knew a local Air National Guard unit would soon deploy to Europe.

She contacted a friend who worked for a local newspaper to write a story. Monday morning the story appeared with the headline, "Baby-deforming Drug May Cost Woman Her Child Here." Reading this headline and knowing that

Sherri's scheduled appointment for an abortion was walking on the edge of Arizona law, hospital administrators and doctors, where Sherri's abortion had been scheduled, cancelled the procedure.

Sherri's story soon caught national as well as international attention, and the Finkbines began receiving death threats, eventually yielding FBI protection. Turning to options outside Arizona, Sherri sought and was turned down for an abortion in Japan. Time was running out when Sherri finally secured an abortion in Sweden during the fourth month of pregnancy.

Following the procedure, the doctor in Sweden informed Sherri that her child would likely not have survived. In the aftermath, due to public reaction, both Sherri and her husband lost their jobs, with Sherri being informed that her television contract was being terminated because she was no longer fit to handle children. With the publicity, lost jobs, and accompanying personal turmoil, the Finkbines' ordeal marked a turning point. A diffuse dissatisfaction with abortion laws across the country began to coalesce into a broad-based movement for change.

Giving further strength to this movement was a pandemic outbreak of rubella across Europe and the United States two years later, between 1964 and 1966. Twenty years earlier, it had been noted that when contracted during pregnancy, rubella was associated with infants being born with a wide range of abnormalities, including deafness and glaucoma, as well as mortality rates approaching 10%–15%. A group of well-respected physicians in San Francisco responded and were performing abortions for mothers exposed to rubella.[28]

The issue came to a head when an anti-abortion leader of the California Board of Medical Examiners began proceedings to revoke the licenses of the nine doctors, soon known as the "San Francisco Nine." A spokesman for the nine doctors responded. The California law was unjust and out of date. The nine doctors, he reported, "did not believe that violation of an archaic statute is unprofessional conduct." A legislative battle was about to unfold.

San Francisco Nine

In June 1966, three pregnant women were scheduled to receive abortions by two doctors at a San Francisco hospital. Each of the women had contracted rubella (German measles) early in their pregnancies. Out of fear of bearing children with birth defects, each had decided to terminate their pregnancies. One of the women already had a disabled child and felt she would be unable to care for two. Though abortion was legal in California at the time, it could only be performed to save a woman's life, not to prevent the birth of a disabled child or to end a pregnancy that was the result of rape.

Eventually the original two doctors were joined by seven others, all facing disciplinary hearings from the State Board of Medical Examiners for their roles in performing technically illegal abortions. Though all the abortions the doctors had performed occurred in a hospital, with informed consent, with approval from the hospitals' abortion committees, and with concurring opinions of other doctors, it was the members of the San Francisco Nine that faced charges of unprofessional conduct and risked the suspension of their medical licenses.

The plight of the San Francisco Nine Fight received extensive media coverage; supporters, including other doctors, lawyers, judges, and religious leaders, formed the California Committee on Therapeutic Abortion, which raised thousands of dollars to help the San Francisco Nine with their legal fees.

Two occurrences delayed the initial hearings of the San Francisco Nine: (1) A case brought before the California Supreme Court asking the court to decide if the doctors had a right to examine the evidence against them. The Medical Board said no; the California Court disagreed. (2) The California legislature was considering changes to the state's abortion laws. In 1967, then-Governor Ronald Reagan signed a new law that expanded abortion access in the state, with one important exception: preventing the birth of a disabled child.

As a result, the Medical Board resumed its hearing against the San Francisco Nine. All of the doctors were found to have engaged in unprofessional conduct, were publicly reprimanded, and were placed on probation. Then, in 1968, a Superior Court judge reversed the Medical Board's decision, arguing that it was unconstitutional to refuse abortion to a woman with high chances of having a disabled child.[29]

Lines were drawn, sides coalesced, and competing legislation was crafted. In California, they were working with a law in effect since 1959. It was restrictive but permitted abortions when the pregnancy involved a substantial risk to the physical or mental health of the mother, when there was a risk of congenital defects, and when the pregnancy was the result of rape, incest, or other types of "felonious intercourse." Sherri Finkbine's case in 1962, along with the Rubella Pandemic and publicity surrounding the "San Francisco Nine," crystallized reform efforts nationwide.[30]

On the anti-abortion side, the Catholic Church remained in strong opposition to abortion in any form. On the other side, the Women's Movement, eventually yielding NOW, was becoming a major counterweight. As one pro-choice activist put it: Without the right to choose to terminate pregnancy, women "would have about as many rights as the cow in the pasture that's taken to the bull once a year . . . if you can't control your own body, you can't control your future."[31]

By the early 1970s, Supreme Court Justices were paying attention, and a case was taking shape in Texas with the lead lawyer, Sarah Weddington. Sherri would later report, "Sarah Weddington would say to me, 'you made my job much easier,' Her job, being of course arguing Roe v. Wade successfully before the Supreme Court!"[32] With the right to privacy set, public opinion awakened, and a case being appealed, the stage was set for the historic, agenda-setting 1973 Supreme Court decision, *Roe v. Wade.*

A Bolt From the Blue: *Roe v. Wade*

Galvanizing events occur from time to time. They shift perspectives and coa- lesce forces. The 9/11 attack on the World Trade Center is one such event. The *Roe v. Wade* decision is another. There were many factors affecting the Supreme Court Justices as they debated the constitutionality of abortion laws, but Sherri Finkbine's plight and the moral dilemmas infusing the rubella pandemic and the "San Francisco Nine" were central. A battle over the legal standing of abortion, as defined by the Supreme Court, and perceptions of the appropriate balance when resolving moral dilemmas infused in the abortion question was about to unfold.

At the time, there were numerous nationwide organizations joining forces to lobby for less restrictive abortion laws. By 1972, the year preceding *Roe,* some 16 states had passed permissive abortion laws based on a template proposed by the Model Penal Code (MPC) and the American Law Institute (ALI).[33] If the abortion was performed by a licensed physician, four states permitted what amounted to "abortion on demand," that is, an abortion at the woman's request without needing medical approval or to prove special circumstances. Forces counterbalancing this trend were largely in the wings (with the impor- tant exception of the Catholic Church). They were about to coalesce and move center stage.

Model Penal Code and Abortion

Except for crimes that relate to a special federal interest (e.g., crimes that occur on federal property or against federal employees, or crimes that cross state lines), states are responsible for establishing their own systems for defining and addressing crime. Rather than a single American criminal legal system, the nation has at least 52 systems—one federal, one for each of the 50 states, and one in Washington, D.C.

In the mid-20th century, the ALI, a non-governmental organization made up of prominent members of the American legal community, was keenly interested in reducing the uncertainty and complexity of the law by making state systems more uniform.[34] In 1951, with funding from the Rockefeller Foundation, the ALI set out to establish a "model" criminal code for US states. After a decade of work, ALI published its "Model Penal Code" (MPC). In the 1960s and 1970s, the MPC was highly influential—many states reformed their criminal codes, and judges often referenced the MPC in their legal decisions.[35]

The drafters of the MPC used a "sociological jurisprudential approach" (i.e., one that considers the actual social effects of law and legal practices).[36] The resulting proposed abortion code considered several "salient features" of abortion practices at the time, including information about the number of abortions, the number of women who die from abortions, who is performing abortions, patterns in violations of abortion law by California hospitals, and other countries' experiences with abortion (specifically those of Denmark and Sweden), among other considerations.[37]

In the code, abortion is framed as a potentially life-saving practice, but the primary emphasis is on the life of the woman rather than the fetus, which the code describes as an "inchoate being." The code made abortion lawful under the following circumstances:

- When performed by a licensed physician in a licensed hospital (unless it is an emergency and/or a licensed hospital is too far away)
- When one more of the following conditions is present:
  - The physical or mental health of the mother will be "gravely" impaired" by the continued pregnancy.
  - The child would be born with a grave physical or mental defect.
  - The pregnancy was the result of rape, incest, or other "felonious intercourse" (e.g., any intercourse with a girl below the age of 16).

The code does not identify a period of time after which an abortion becomes illegal, but it does recommend increasing the severity of the offense after 26 weeks. The 26-week marker is identified as important because of the increased risks to the health of the woman of an abortion later in pregnancy rather than the developmental stage of the fetus. Finally, the code explicitly states that the use of contraception, including those that prevent implantation after fertilization, is not regulated by the code.[38]

In 1973, *Roe v. Wade* came, as one observer put it, like a bolt from the blue.[39] The Supreme Court, drawing on the contraception cases just decided and voting 7-2, declared the prohibition of abortion was unconstitutional. In the early stages of their discussions, Justice Potter Stewart, along with several of his colleagues, worked under the flawed assumption that the case would be easily resolved. Justice Blackmun would later note, "How wrong we were."[40] Eventually, Supreme Court Justices framed their historic decision by reemphasizing the right to privacy as established in the two contraception cases. They weighed the protection of evolving fetal life against the mother's life, health, and right to privacy and came up with a sliding scale to balance competing moral questions.

The newly conceived fetus, the Court decided, was not a constitutionally protected person. Abortion was not to be prohibited in early gestation. It should be left to the discretion of the expectant mother to decide. As gestation progressed, however, fetal personhood began to emerge and develop. Constitutional rights and duties shifted. The fetus began to take on characteristics of a constitutionally protected person as it became viable, capable of living outside the mother's womb. At the time, fetal viability was set at between 24 and 28 weeks, or as the pregnancy entered the final three months.

Timing of Abortion: Trimesters and Fetal Development[41]

Many of the laws regulating abortion delineate a legal abortion from an illegal one based on certain developmental aspects of the fetus (e.g., presence of a "heartbeat."). Even those laws that specify a particular week tend to do so based on the belief that the fetus has achieved a specific development milestone that week.

Though not commonly used today, some older abortion laws identify "quickening" as the marker for when an abortion becomes illegal. Quickening is when the woman first feels the movement of the fetus. Detection of fetal movement is subjective and appears to vary based on whether the woman has had previous pregnancies. Women have reported first feeling fetal movement anywhere from 13 to 25 weeks.

The more common contemporary marker is that of "viability," generally defined as when there is a reasonable likelihood of sustained survival outside of the womb with or without artificial support.

Fetal viability varies from fetus to fetus and is never certain, even in seemingly healthy pregnancies. Rather than a guarantee, viability is a probability, though sometimes a difficult one to estimate precisely.

Many factors contribute to fetus viability, including considerations specific to the fetus such as gestational age (GA), weight, and sex (female fetuses fare better than males); conditions specific to the woman, such as environment, health, nutrition, and genetic factors; and circumstances specific to the region, such as availability of medical interventions (i.e., a nearby hospital with a NICU unit), access to, and stipulations of insurance providers, and hospital-specific definitions of viability. In short, it could be true that two fetuses at the same GA may not both be deemed viable, or that the same fetus could be deemed viable in one region of the country but not in another.

Some of the newly emerging abortion laws have moved away from using viability as the important marker and, instead, rely on a seemingly more specific characteristic of the fetal development. Typically, pregnancy is tracked by "gestational age" (GA), which begins on the first day of the last menstrual cycle, approximately two weeks before fertilization occurs. In other words, during the first two weeks of "pregnancy," the woman is not yet pregnant.

The chart below lists the GAs at which key developmental characteristics of the embryo/fetus typically occur within healthy pregnancies. These characteristics have been selected based on those that have emerged as important in the ongoing abortion debate.

Embryo/Fetal Development by Gestational Age

Gestational Age	Developmental Description
Week 3	Egg and sperm unite in the fallopian tube to form zygote (fertilization); zygote begins travel to the uterus.
Week 4	The ball of cells (blastocyst) about the size of a poppy seed burrows into the uterine lining (implantation).
Week 5	Hormone levels increase enough to stop menstrual period— often the first sign of pregnancy for someone who has regular periods; an embryo is about the size of a sesame seed.
Week 6	Organs, including the heart, begin to form; the presence of cardiac activity can be detected; the embryo is about the size of a lentil.
Week 10	End of embryonic development/start of fetus stage; major organs are formed and continue to develop; cartilage, bones, nails, and hair begin appearing; the fetus is about the size of a cherry tomato.
Week 17	The four chambers of the heart have developed, and a heartbeat can be detected[42]; the fetus is about the size of a pear.
Week 24	Fetus has the necessary nerve and brain development to perceive pain; fetus viability is presumed at this point.
Week 31	Fetus has finished most of its major development; focus is on gaining weight.
Week 40	Birth of fetus

With viability established as the touchstone marking the last three months of pregnancy, the Justices decided to divide the gestation process into three-month periods, or trimesters. The decision to terminate the pregnancy was solely at the discretion of the woman in consultation with her physician during the first three months. During the next three months, the state could regulate abortion procedures (but not outlaw) in the interests of the mother's health. During the final three months, the state could regulate or outlaw what came to be known as "late-term" abortions, except when necessary to preserve the health or life of the mother. The Court's decision with its roughly hewn trimesters would eventually produce a debate infused with a fury not altogether anticipated.

The Court released the *Roe* decision on Monday, January 22, 1973, two days after President Nixon was inaugurated. It was a momentous day. In addition to being the day when the boundaries of legal abortion were redefined, it was the day President Lyndon B. Johnson died as well as the day Henry Kissinger flew to Paris to finalize the end of the Vietnam War. Fifty years later, January 22, 1973, would be headlined as "The day that changed America."[43] On this day, cheers were heard from supporters of the right to choose. These cheers were greeted by equally vocal opposition—more people joined various anti-abortion groups in 1973 than in any other year. The cultural wars were about to begin.

By the time the 1973 decision was released, the seven concurring Supreme Court Justices knew well they were treading on sensitive, contentious ground. Writing for the majority, Justice Blackmun stated:

> We forthwith acknowledge our awareness of the sensitive and emotional nature of the abortion controversy, of the vigorous opposing views, even among physicians, and of the deep and seemingly absolute convictions that the subject inspires. One's philosophy, one's experiences, one's exposure to the raw edges of human existence, one's religious training, one's attitudes toward life and family and their values, and the moral standards one establishes and seeks to observe, are all likely to influence and to color one's thinking and conclusions about abortion.

These standards, attitudes, and emotions, Blackmun continued, should be set aside. The Court should "resolve the issue by constitutional measurement, free of emotion." Did laws prohibiting abortion violate the Constitution? That was the single question. Blackmun and six of his colleagues found that they did. From January 22, 1973, onward, *Roe v. Wade* was the law of the land.

Questioning the legitimacy of the *Roe* decision was immediate. Importantly, an article appeared three months later in *The Yale Law Journal* written by a well-respected legal scholar, John Hart Ely.[44] Ely's article soon became one of the most widely cited pieces in the history of the *Journal*. Interestingly, the article would be cited 50 years later by Justice Alito when Roe was overturned. For Ely, the question of abortion posed heartbreaking moral dilemmas. He agreed with the substance of the decision the Court had released. His disagreement was with who was deciding. The Supreme Court, he argued, was for all intents and purposes drafting legislation. They should not be engaged in this activity. This was the job of state legislatures. It was an argument heard again and again over the coming decades and would be a lynchpin when *Dobbs* overruled *Roe* a half-century later.

The Power of Empathy: The Personhood of the Fetus

Much of the *Roe* Court's decision turned on the idea that the early-term fetus was not a person under the Constitution and thus did not have the attendant protections. Many found it hard to accept this cornerstone. Instead, anti-abortion advocates sought to arouse empathy for the fetus by showing and publicizing intrauterine images as well as graphic photos of late-term aborted fetal tissue. After seeing the fetus moving in the womb, how could you deny the fetus being a person? Particularly important was the film *The Silent Scream*,[45] produced by Dr. Bernard Nathanson, an obstetrician-gynecologist and former director of the largest abortion clinic in New York City and perhaps the Western world.

Nathanson eventually wrote a book, *The Hand of God*, in which he stated, "When ultrasound in the early 1970s confronted me with the sight of the embryo in the womb, I simply lost my faith in abortion on demand."[46] He had been shaken to "the very roots of his soul" by what he saw and had stopped performing abortions.

The Silent Scream was greeted with mixed reviews. For some, it was mind opening, empathy-generating, and conscience-prodding. It was praised for raising public awareness of the tragedy of abortion. The short film was likened to Harriet Beecher Stowe's *Uncle Tom's Cabin*, which had revealed the evils of slavery. Life is sacred. The fetus was a small, developing human being. How could we legalize the tearing apart of a human being?

For others, the film was scientifically inaccurate, technical flimflam, a misrepresentation of the early-term fetus. Shameful exploitation. For these viewers, the film was nothing more than an intentionally flawed piece of propaganda. Eventually, a major television network ran a program with several prominent physicians from across the nation decrying the film's flaws.[47] Most importantly, the critics claimed, the "silent scream" was simply a fetal reflex. Whatever the film's accuracy, President Ronald Reagan, who had recently published "Abortion and the Conscience of the Nation," had the film screened in the White House and subsequently provided the film to members of Congress. In the end, religious leaders held screenings across the nation.

Dismantling *Roe*: Shifting Composition of the Supreme Court

As Ronald Reagan's time in office ended, the composition and leadership of the Supreme Court had shifted. President Reagan had elevated a Chief Justice and had three nominations of Supreme Court Justices confirmed. By most assessments, the *Roe* 7-2 majority was now closer to 5-4 when it came to the constitutional standing of abortion. As presidential appointments altered the balance of the Court, there were several cases testing whether the 1973 *Roe* decision would stand, but none more important than the 1989 *Webster v. Reproductive Health Services* case and the 1992 decision, *Planned Parenthood of Southeastern Pennsylvania v. Casey.*

In 1986, Missouri passed a law prohibiting the use of public resources for abortion counseling or provision. The preamble to the law included the statement, "The life of each human being begins at conception." In *Webster,* the Supreme Court addressed several provisions of the Missouri statute. Though the Court's reasoning was divided across provisions, pluralities wrote in support of the *state's* ability to regulate the performance of abortion. And, in one controversial and perhaps telling move, the Court refused to invalidate Missouri law's preamble. While, in the end, the center held and *Roe* was not overturned, the *Webster* decision was a sign of changes to come.

One key change was that several Justices found the trimester framework unsound in principle and unworkable in practice. They argued it should be abandoned.

> *Roe's* rigid trimester analysis has proved to be unsound in principle and unworkable in practice. . . . The *Roe* framework is hardly consistent with the notion of a constitution like ours that is cast in general terms and usually speaks in general principles. The framework's key elements—trimesters and viability—are not found in the Constitution's text, . . . the result has been a web of legal rules that have become increasingly intricate, resembling a code of regulations, rather than a body of constitutional doctrine. There is also no reason why the State's compelling interest in protecting potential human life should not extend throughout pregnancy, rather than coming into existence only at the point of viability. Thus, the *Roe* trimester framework should be abandoned.

It was a bold decision, attracting a good deal of commentary, both positive and negative, both in and outside the legal profession. Still, *Roe* remained the law of the land.

Writing with only partially veiled disappointment and a hint of disdain, Justice Scalia, in his concurring statement, wrote, "It thus appears that the mansion of constitutionalized abortion law, constructed overnight in *Roe v. Wade,* must be disassembled doorjamb by doorjamb, and never entirely brought down, no matter how wrong it may be." To say the least, tension remained.

Three years later, the Court handed down its 1992 decision in a case from Pennsylvania, *Planned Parenthood of Southeastern Pennsylvania v. Casey.* The Pennsylvania legislature had amended its law to require: (1) informed consent about potential negative impacts of abortion on the woman's health; (2) a

24-hour waiting period prior to the abortion procedure; (3) consent from at least one parent when the person seeking an abortion was a minor; and (4) notification of the husband when a married woman was seeking an abortion.

For foes, these provisions were seen as burdensome requirements designed to delay and discourage. The Supreme Court partially agreed, writing that the Pennsylvania legislature had crafted an "undue burden" for a woman seeking an abortion.

In a rare step, the opinion for the Court was crafted and authored by three justices: O'Connor, Kennedy, and Souter. Justice Sandra Day O'Conner summed up the Court's finding: "We are led to conclude this: the essential holding of *Roe v. Wade* should be retained and once again affirmed." Though the Court had again reaffirmed the "essential holding" of *Roe* in their bitter 5-to-4 decision, their decision allowed for new hurdles to be created. Other than the provision that husbands must be notified, the Court upheld the other Pennsylvania provisions. In addition, the justices largely abandoned the trimester framework and, instead, argued states can regulate abortion based on fetal viability—state interests increase and women's interests decrease as the fetus develops. The door to challenge *Roe* is nudged open a bit more.

Protests and Violent Opposition

By this time, numerous activist organizations had formed. Several of these equated abortion with murder. Protests and disruptive actions, some violent, even fatal, followed. Clinics were targeted with blockages, arson, and bombings; providers received death threats, and some were murdered.[48]

One such organization, Operation Rescue,[49] *adopted the slogan: "If You Believe Abortion is Murder, Act like it*'s Murder." Another was the Pro-Life Action League (PLAL). PLAL published a how-to book on closing clinics and stopping providers titled *Closed: 99 Ways to Stop Abortion*. This how-to book stated as a premise:

No social movement in the history of this country has succeeded without activist(s) taking to the streets. Activism . . . is necessary not only to save lives, but to garner public attention, bring media into the struggle, and shake politicians into recognizing the determination of anti-abortion supporters.[50]

The lines between God's will and man's law were being drawn. Following a protest at the 1988 Democratic National Convention in Atlanta, Georgia, the leader of Operation Rescue was quoted as saying, "God never gave the Government a blank check to do what it wants to do. It is heresy to teach Christians to obey the law which runs counter to His law."[51] For some, such as the Army of God and Rescue America, an outgrowth of Operation Rescue, this logic justified violence and the taking of lives to save lives.

On March 10, 1993, a little over two months after the twentieth anniversary of *Roe*, Dr. David Gunn, who was providing abortion services in Alabama, Florida, and Georgia, became the first abortion provider shot and killed by an avid anti-abortion advocate. Michael Griffin, the shooter, had been influenced by what his attorneys characterized as relentless badgering and the showing of graphic images at church meetings by his minister, a local anti-abortion extremist and former Ku Klux Klan member.[52] Two months later, Dr. George Tiller, the primary focus of the Summer of Mercy protests, was shot and wounded in a botched attempt on his life by Shelley Shannon, also a participant in the Summer of Mercy and a supporter of Michael Griffin.

Summer of Mercy

For much of the 1960s through the 1980s, Kansas was one of the most liberal states with respect to abortion—state Republicans had passed laws allowing for abortion in the cases of rape, incest, threats to maternal health, and fetal deformity. Perhaps more important, it was one of only three states that had no regulation of abortion in the second or third trimesters. As a result, it was common for women from nearby states, including Missouri, Oklahoma, and Nebraska, to travel to Kansas to obtain an abortion. After *Roe,* Kansans were more supportive of elective abortion than the rest of the nation—only about 25% were against abortion. And, until the late 1980s, political officials of both parties avoided abortion-related legislation, operating under an informal agreement to table abortion bills to avoid having to publicly vote on them.

Though a relatively liberal state, there was a small but growing contingent of antiabortion activists. Local activists were becoming increasingly vocal but were still quite fractured in the early 1980s—incrementalists were more pragmatic in their advocacy, attempting to chip away at abortion laws gradually, while purists advocated for banning the practice altogether. By the late 1980s, these two groups found common ground in model legislation that defined a fetus as a person from conception—in finding agreement on the personhood of a fetus, they could shift focus away from disagreements about which specific legislative strategies were best. However, like abortion activists in other states, Kansan activists were increasingly discouraged about the slow pace of change at the legislative level—they became frustrated over waiting to "save all babies" and, instead, opted for direct action as a means to save "just a few." The shift to direct action (e.g., prayer circles outside clinics, clinic blockades) resulted in an influx of the state's fundamental and evangelical Christians, for whom such public displays were inherently appealing.

While activists targeted each of the Wichita's three clinics, the bulk of activist and media attention was on the Women's Health Care Services clinic, where George Tiller had worked since 1975. Tiller was one of three providers in the nation who performed abortions in the third trimester. He had become a physician after learning his father provided abortions during the "criminal era," when abortion was illegal. Tiller advertised in medical journals and at medical conventions; to the ire of activists, his advertisements often included the prices of abortion, which would increase later in the pregnancy. For patients who traveled from distant areas, Tiller worked out arrangements with local hotels for reduced costs for lodging; if they couldn't afford or find lodging, he would let them stay at his house.

At the start of the Summer of Mercy, police had convinced physicians at all three of the local clinics to temporarily shut down their operations in anticipation of the protests. News of the week-long shutdown became a popular topic in the national media and on activist hotlines. Inspired by the success, protesters from other parts of Kansas and from nearby states traveled to join the activities. Local activists opened their homes to the out-of-towners. By the end of the six weeks of protest, 1,781 people were arrested 2,753 times (many individuals were arrested multiple times). Local and national antiabortion groups saw both their membership and their revenues swell.

By 1992, Kansas changed its abortion law to become more restrictive and to make it illegal to block clinics.[53] At the time the legislation was passed, there were 15 abortion providers in the state. By 2005, there were seven. The local activists who were catalyzed by the Summer of Mercy then expanded their attention to the teaching of evolution and of sex education in schools.[54]

These actions, along with the history of clinic blockades, arson, kidnappings, assaults, chemical attacks, and more, prodded many to seek additional legal protections for clinics and providers. In May 1994, on a bipartisan vote, the Freedom of Access to Clinic Entrances (FACE) Act was passed by the US Congress and signed into law by President Clinton.[55] FACE made it a federal crime to "physically obstruct the entrance to a clinic or to use force, the threat of force, or physical obstruction, such as a sit-in, to interfere with, injure, or intimidate clinic workers or women seeking abortions or other reproductive health services."

The FACE Act was an important piece of legislation. It did not, however, end the violence. Two months later, on July 29, 1994, another anti-abortion protester and former Presbyterian minister, Paul Hill, drawing on his beliefs about God's will and its supremacy over the Supreme Court and other manmade laws, shot and killed Dr. John Britton along with his armed escort. Dr. Britton had been

Chart of Violence at Reproductive Health Clinics[56]

Type of Incident	Number of Incidents					
	1977 to 1989	1990s	2000s	2010s	2020 to 2022	Total
Murder (Including Attempted)	0	23	2	12	0	37
Kidnapping	2	1	1	0	0	4
Assault and Battery	58	53	71	132	217	531
Stalking		404	110	106	124	744
Bombing/Arson (Including Attempted)	184	203	106	152	234	879
Trespassing/Invasion	247	310	1,889	4,393	2,680	9,519
Picketing/Obstruction	847	29,937	110,600	421,514	348,947	911,845
Burglary/Vandalism	264	610	668	699	368	2,609
Bioterrorism	0	147	614	2	4	767
Bomb/Death Threats	307	492	217	402	624	2,042
Hate Mail/Suspicious Packages	192	6,327	6,715	137,282	78,433	228,949
Total	3,585	69,661	234,799	991,322	783,647	2,083,014

recruited to carry on the work of Dr. Gunn in providing abortion services in Pensacola, Florida. While Paul Hill sat in prison, there was more violence, additional killings related to anti-abortion protesters, as well as heated exchanges and political campaigns debating the right to choose abortion. After nine years on Florida's death row, Paul Hill became the first person, on September 3, 2003, executed for killing an abortion provider.

Late-Term Abortions

Even Paul Hill's execution, however, did not end the violence. On May 31, 2009, Dr. George Tiller, the physician wounded by Shelley Shannon following the Summer of Mercy demonstrations, was shot and killed by another anti-abortion activist, Scott Roeder. At the time, Dr. Tiller, who ran an abortion clinic providing late-term abortions (i.e., during the third trimester), was serving as an usher at his Lutheran Church in Wichita, Kansas. The next day, Randall Terry, founder of Operation Rescue, again invoking God's law, was quoted as saying:

> George Tiller was a mass-murderer. We grieve for him that he did not have time to properly prepare his soul to face God. I am more concerned that the Obama Administration will use Tiller's killing to intimidate pro-lifers into surrendering our most effective rhetoric and actions. Abortion is still murder. And we still must call abortion by its proper name: murder.

Those men and women who slaughter the unborn are murderers according to the Law of God. We must continue to expose them in our communities and peacefully protest them at their offices and homes, and yes, even their churches.[57]

Dr. Tiller had been the focus of animosity among those opposed to abortion due to his nationally advertised services for late-term abortions. Though they inspired a great deal of concern, third trimester abortions were quite rare. Most estimates put the number of abortions occurring at 21 weeks or more of gestation at close to 1% or less of the total number of abortions carried out in the nation.[58]

Abortions Later in Pregnancy[59]

Practitioners use the term "abortion later in pregnancy" rather than terms more commonly used by activists and media, including "late-term abortion," "dismemberment," "partial-birth abortion," "post-birth abortion," "born-alive abortion," and "post-viability abortion."[60] Because these terms collapse abortions that occur in the second and third trimesters, some practitioners prefer to use a more specific description, "abortion at 20 weeks of gestation." Providers generally define an abortion later in pregnancy as one that occurs at greater than 21 weeks. This cutoff, however, is determined more by how data is collected by the Centers for Disease Control, rather than a medical consideration.

Abortions later in pregnancy are rare, costly, and time-intensive. Currently, there are only four publicly known providers that offer third-trimester abortions.[61] Annually, approximately 0.02% of all abortions (or 320 to 600 cases) occur after 26 weeks.[62]

There are three primary reasons for seeking abortions in the late stages of gestation:

- Fetal life-threatening abnormalities: While a few serious genetic conditions, such as trisomy disorders (e.g., Down syndrome) and cystic fibrosis, can be detected as early as ten weeks, many other abnormalities are detected late in the pregnancy. Fetal anomaly testing, which looks at fetal organ development, typically occurs around 20 weeks. Most of those who learn of serious fetal anomalies at this stage choose to terminate their pregnancy, even when these pregnancies were wanted.
- Danger to the mother's health: This can include maternal cancer, preeclampsia, premature rupture of the amniotic sac, and intrauterine infections.
- Delays in obtaining an earlier abortion: lack of access to nearby facilities, lack of insurance coverage, inability to pay out of pocket, and health conditions with similar symptoms to pregnancy resulting in women not knowing they were pregnant until later in their pregnancy.[63]

Concern about late-term abortions did not begin with the services provided by Dr. Tiller. It had been around for many years. In recent decades, it was noted in the oral arguments in *Roe v. Wade* when justices Marshall and Stewart discussed late-term abortions with Robert Flowers, assistant attorney general for the State of Texas:

Mr. Justice Stewart:	That it is an offense to a kill a child in the process of childbirth.
Mr. Flowers:	Yes, sir. It would be immediately before childbirth or right in the proximity of the child being born.
Mr. Justice Marshall:	Which is not an abortion.
Mr. Flowers:	Which is not—would not be an abortion. Yes, sir, you're correct, sir. It would be homicide.[64]

In 1995, there were federal legislative efforts to limit late-term abortions. For supporters, the case was compelling:

> To think that a human being would actually hold a little baby in his or her hand, and then kill it—that's what got me, . . . If you're holding that child in your hand, and knowingly killing the child, you can't argue anymore that it's not really a human being. You just can't do it.[65]

The proposed law had strong support in both the US House (288–139) and Senate (54–44). There were not, however, enough votes to override a presidential veto, which was forthcoming. In announcing his veto, President Clinton anchored his opposition in the Act's lack of attention to "serious adverse health consequences" for the mother.

At the veto signing, President Clinton met with five women and their families he had invited to the ceremony in early April 1996.[66] They came from different religious faiths, different political parties, and had differing views on abortion. There was, however, some common ground. They all desperately wanted their child, and they did not want to have an abortion. Finally, they all had been confronted with agonizing decisions. These decisions were made "only when it became clear that their babies would not survive, their own lives, their health, and in some cases, their capacity to have children in the future were in danger."

The first mother to speak was a "practicing Catholic." She and her husband were overjoyed with the news she was pregnant with their first child. Then, as she entered the fifth month of gestation, an ultrasound indicated a problem:

> The diagnosis was as bad as it could be. Our little boy had a very advanced text-book case of hydrocephaly. All the doctors told us there was no hope. We asked about in utero surgery, about shunts to remove the fluid, but there was absolutely nothing we could do. I cannot express the pain we still feel. . . . Not only

was our son going to die, but the complications of the pregnancy put my health in danger, as well. . . . Several specialists recommended that we terminate the pregnancy. I thank God every day that I had this safe medical option available to me, especially now that I am pregnant again and expecting a baby in September.

The next woman to speak was, in her words, a conservative Republican "extremely opposed" to abortion:

I found out when I was seven months pregnant that my daughter was dying. She was dying inside my womb. . . . For three weeks we attempted to turn my daughter so that I could deliver her vaginally and naturally. We had one hope, and that was that we would be able to hold our daughter alive for possibly an hour, maybe two. . . . She was dying and she would likely not survive any labor and there was no way I could deliver her. We had her baptized in utero. . . . This is not about abortion, and it's not about choice. It's a medical issue.

Three additional mothers spoke similarly of their own heart wrenching experiences, expressing their wonderment over the lack of provision for health-based exceptions in the proposed law.

In closing, President Clinton turned his attention to Congress and the specific flaws he saw in the legislation he was vetoing.

If you want to pass something on this procedure, let's make an exception for life and serious adverse health consequences so that we don't put these women in a position and these families in a position where they will lose all possibility of future childbearing, or where the doctor can't say that they might die, but they could clearly be substantially injured forever. . . . I will say again, if the Congress really wants to act out of a sincere concern that some of these things are done, . . . then if they will meet my standards to protect these families, they could pass a bill that I would sign tomorrow.

With a presidential veto in place, some states began crafting their own laws. These were challenged in numerous federal courts.

The first to wind its way to the Supreme Court came from Nebraska. In Nebraska's case, the law was challenged two days after passage. Several months later, on June 28, 2000, the Supreme Court delivered an aggressively argued 5-4 decision, *Stenberg v. Carhart,* declaring the Nebraska law unconstitutional.

The 5-4 decision was written aggressively on both sides. The five justices in the majority focused a good deal of their attention on the lack of an exception for the mother's health. There were also ambiguities seen in the description of prohibited or permitted abortion procedures. The bill referred to a "substantial portion" of the fetus being in the vagina. What did this mean? A foot? A leg? The torso? It was unclear.

There was too much ambiguity in what was allowed and what was prohibited. This put both the mother and physician at legal risk. The law, taken as a whole, presented an "undue burden" and thus violated the *Casey* decision. It was, therefore, held to be unconstitutional. There were similar problems in two dozen other laws that had been passed. These too were unconstitutional. It was a serious setback for those working to ban partial birth abortions. The battle, however, was not over.

George W. Bush's election was certified a half year after the Supreme Court declared Nebraska's law unconstitutional. His administration would soon become consumed with the attack on the World Trade Center, but his supporters knew well the new president was far more sympathetic to banning abortions than his predecessor. Laws were drafted, hearings and debates held, and votes taken. On November 5, President Bush signed the Partial Birth Abortion Act of 2003 into law. The question became, would this Act be approved by the Supreme Court?

While it did not include exceptions for the mother's health, the new Act did clarify the procedural ambiguity that bothered Justices when declaring the earlier Nebraska statute unconstitutional. In signing the Act, President Bush noted with satisfaction, "The bill I am about to sign protecting innocent new life from this practice reflects the compassion and humanity of America." There was optimism that Court approval would be forthcoming.

Given the lack of attention to the mother's health, however, the question remained whether the Act would survive Supreme Court review now that the Nebraska case was in place. It was clear that Congress intended to exclude consideration of all health issues. The first paragraph of the Act read, "A moral, medical, and ethical consensus exists that the practice of performing a partial-birth abortion . . . is never medically necessary and should be prohibited." The problem was that there was no consensus. The mothers speaking at President Clinton's announcement of his veto would disagree, as would many members of the medical profession.[67]

A second problem the Supreme Court had found with the Nebraska statute was the ambiguous wording defining a "partial-birth abortion." Drafters of the Act under consideration were careful to address this ambiguity, stating,

> (T)he term "partial-birth abortion" means an abortion in which the person performing the abortion—deliberately and intentionally vaginally delivers a living fetus until, in the case of a head-first presentation, the entire fetal head is outside the body of the mother, or, in the case of breech presentation, any part of the fetal trunk past the navel is outside the body of the mother, for the purpose of performing an overt act that the person knows will kill the partially delivered living fetus.

Head-first and breech birth markers were now specified. It was the fetal head or trunk of the infant's body, depending on orientation. The appeals started immediately.

The same day President Bush signed the Act, appeals challenging the new law were filed in Northern California, Southern New York, and Nebraska. The resulting court decisions were not good news for supporters of the Act. By 2006, the Partial Birth Abortion Act of 2003 was held unconstitutional in six lower federal courts. As expected, with reference to the Nebraska case, most problematic was the Act's silence on exceptions for the mother's health. This flew in the face of the Supreme Court's decision in *Stenberg*. But the vote in this case had been 5-4. Given the close vote and a shifting membership on the Supreme Court, and despite the consensus in lower courts declaring the Act unconstitutional, there was hope the 2003 Act would be approved by the reshaped Supreme Court. Consistent with this hopeful optimism, Justices agreed to hear the cases from Nebraska and California in February 2006.[68]

Despite the lack of provisions for considering the mother's health, this time Justices voted (5-4) to approve the 2003 Act, again in heated disagreement. The case, *Gonzales v. Carhart*,[69] was considered one of the most important abortion decisions in the past 30 years. There was much applause. There was also distress. The president of the American College of Obstetricians and Gynecologists declared that the decision "leaves no doubt that women's health in America is perceived as being of little consequence." Whatever the support or opposition, the Partial-Birth Abortion Act of 2003 was now the law of the land.

Physicians, mothers, and hospitals adjusted. A few months after the decision was announced, an article ran in the Boston Globe reporting adjustments by abortion providers in and around Boston.[70] To make sure they did not violate the procedures specified in the Act, physicians were injecting the fetus with lethal drugs prior to its passage into the mother's vagina. What was accomplished? The child would be without life before entering the birth canal. The specified markers were no longer at risk of being violated. Three Boston hospitals had responded "by making the injections the new standard operating procedure for abortions beginning at around 20 weeks' gestation. . . . No physician even wants to be accused of stumbling into accidentally doing one of these (prohibited) procedures." It was a strange and strained moment.

Modern Abortion Methods

Most modern abortions are completed by taking medicine or by undergoing a procedure (which also may involve the taking of abortion medication.)[71] More than half of all contemporary abortions are medication abortions that occur within the first ten weeks of pregnancy. For a medication abortion, a patient first takes mifepristone (RU-486) which blocks progesterone, a hormone needed for a pregnancy to continue. Within a day or two, the patient then takes misoprostol, a drug that causes the uterus to contract and empty. There are few complications with this method of abortion. As a result, in some jurisdictions, patients can administer the drugs themselves.

Vacuum aspirations are procedural abortions that usually occur between 6 and 12 weeks of pregnancy. It is a short procedure (5–10 minutes) in which a vacuum tube that is inserted into the uterus gently empties the uterus. Patients are generally awake and may experience cramping as a result of the procedure.

Most abortions that occur in the second trimester are dilation and evacuation abortions (D&E). A few hours before the procedure, patients are typically given medication (often mifepristone and misoprostol) to dilate the cervix. If more dilation is needed, the physician may use dilators to further open the cervix. The physician will then use instruments, which may include forceps and/or a vacuum, to remove the pregnancy. The procedure itself takes 10–20 minutes, but patients often remain at the clinic for additional monitoring.[72]

Inductions take place after 16 weeks of pregnancy. These procedures take place over the course of several days in a hospital. Depending on how far along the pregnancy is, the first step may be an injection to stop the fetal heartbeat. Then medicines will be used to cause the uterus to contract and begin the labor process. The pregnancy is pushed out as a result of this labor process.[73]

Determining Undue Burden

Late-term abortions were not the only issue being debated in the latter decade of the 20th century. Though the Court's decision, *Planned Parenthood of Southeastern Pennsylvania v. Casey,* had upheld *Roe v. Wade* in 1992, it had also opened the door for abortion restrictions. Restrictions could be imposed if they did not present an "undue burden." It was a door anti-abortion advocates charged through, fashioning what eventually came to be known as TRAP (Targeted Regulations of Abortion Providers) laws. If these laws did not violate the "undue burden" test, they could discourage abortion through various restrictive requirements on clinics, providers, and patients. As new items were drafted, passed, and signed into law, they were met with opposition from those looking to limit governmental intervention on a woman's right to choose.[74]

Two decades after *Casey*, a wave of restrictive laws had swept across the nation. It did not seem to be slowing down. Between 2011 and 2013, more laws were passed (205) than in the entire previous decade (189). The range of restrictions was broad, including clinic requirements, mandatory intrauterine ultrasounds, and statements physicians were mandated to use when securing informed consent. These laws were part of a nationwide, coordinated effort aimed at shutting down abortion providers through costly or otherwise burdensome requirements.

The TRAP laws were only one avenue of post-*Casey* attacks on rights defined in *Roe*. Additional laws were proposed and passed. When was there a detectable heartbeat? When did the fetus experience suffering? Why not prohibit abortion at these points? They were easily as important as whether the fetus could survive outside the mother's womb. A detectable heartbeat and the experience of suffering were indicators we could empathize with. Why not consider the fetus a constitutionally protected person at these points?

Prior to 2016, the year the Supreme Court clarified the meaning of "undue burden" in *Whole Woman's Health v. Hellerstedt*.[75] There were an estimated 55 TRAP laws in 34 states.[76] These laws were wide-ranging, affecting such things as clinic room size and the width of hallways, requiring costly renovations. Also present were requirements that clinics be a certain distance from hospitals, making clinic location in rural areas difficult.[77] In addition to requirements related to the architecture and location of clinics, several states focused on mandatory counseling of women seeking an abortion, counseling accompanied by mandated viewing of fetal ultrasounds and specified waiting periods after the viewing. Did these restrictions present an undue burden?

As the mandated sonogram laws went into effect and prior to clarification of the "undue burden" standard, an obvious question emerged: What was the purpose of these laws? Why mandate that a woman view a sonogram and listen to a scripted account of an abortion? Clearly there was an agenda and very little, if any, medical reason for the mandated viewing and scripted counseling.

One of these laws went into effect in Texas in February 2012. National Public Radio ran a program featuring a woman's deeply personal reaction.[78] She noted at the outset that she and her husband had a young daughter at home and were looking forward to bringing a new child into the world. They had visited the doctor to view a sonogram, mainly to determine the gender of the new child and share the excitement.

An unexpected fetal anomaly was detected, and a second voluntary sonogram was requested and taken. Both revealed a developmental problem with their son's spine, brain, and legs. The prognosis was that the child would suffer greatly and need a lifetime of care. Making a heartbreaking decision, the mother and father decided to have an abortion.

Although two sonograms had already been performed, another was required by the recently passed law mandating such viewing 24 hours before the procedure. The abortion provider was also mandated to discuss the decision with the mother, using a predetermined script. Following this disturbing, mandated procedure, the mother decided to publish an article about her experience.[79] She wondered, "What good is a law that adds only pain and difficulty to perhaps the most painful and difficult decision a woman can make?" In her opinion, politicians "wanted women to have the sonograms so that they can see the life of the child that they are about to end, so it is an entirely ideological justification for why a woman would have to have a sonogram." She would also recall, "It was a terrible choice; it was a heart-wrenching one. But it was also a simple one because as his parents, we chose what we believed was best for him, to prevent him from knowing a life of pain."

Texas was not alone. Additional sonogram laws in other states were drafted, passed, and appealed. These laws involved either transvaginal or "jelly on the belly" ultrasounds. Whether they changed minds is unclear, though as one well-informed observer noted, 60% of abortion seekers had already had a child and that "[w]omen are having abortions because of the conditions of their lives, their economic situation, their partner situation, their age," she continued, "and the ultrasound doesn't change that."[80]

An exchange between the provider and patient illustrates further:

"I've always been uncomfortable with gynecologists," Amy (the patient) says, fidgeting on the examination table.

"I understand," Kathy (the provider) says, preparing the transvaginal probe as Amy stares wide-eyed. "The first step in this process is to perform an ultrasound to determine how far along you are. According to our state law, I must show you the ultrasound and you must hear the fetal heartbeat, if there is one. I know this might be uncomfortable, and I apologize."

"I don't want to see the ultrasound," Amy says. "What the baby looks like doesn't make a difference to me—I am having this abortion because I'm not financially able to support a child right now. Having to see this ultrasound isn't going to change my mind."[81]

And, so, mandated sonograms, mind-changing or not, were required by law and performed.

Returning to architectural and clinic location requirements, two of these were addressed, again in a Texas law requiring abortion clinics to meet the same standards as ambulatory surgical centers and that abortion providers have admitting privileges at a nearby (within 30 miles) hospital. The law was challenged and eventually wound its way to the US Supreme Court by 2016 in the case, *Whole Woman's Health v. Hellerstedt*.

The Court used the occasion not only to decide the case but also to clarify the "undue burden" standard. The Justices found in a 5-3 decision, supported by such organizations as the American Medical Association,[82] that the Texas law did not "confer medical benefits that are sufficient to justify the burdens they impose on women seeking to exercise their constitutional right to an abortion. Therefore, the provisions unconstitutionally impose an undue burden."

Undue burden was an ambiguous standard, not well defined.[83] The Texas law required high-dollar, hospital-level upgrades to clinics as well as requirements for doctors to affiliate with local hospitals, affiliations that were sometimes not very local or impossible to establish. These were clearly burdensome requirements for clinics, doctors, and patients. Were they "undue?"

By the time oral arguments were heard before the Court in 2016, the number of abortion clinics in Texas had fallen to 23, half the number of clinics prior to the legislation and a bit lower than one clinic per one million people. For supporters, this was precisely the intended effect. They applauded. For opponents, the requirements were troubling, expensive, and burdensome. The Supreme Court found the requirements combined to produce an undue burden and were thus unconstitutional.

In its decision to declare the Texas law unconstitutional, the Court noted the need for clarification of what "undue burden" meant. From henceforth, they wrote, courts would be asked to determine if the law in question:

- Furthered a valid state interest. Courts could not defer to state claims in this regard.
- Produced benefits of an abortion restriction that outweighed the burdens it created, and if the burdens outweighed the benefits claimed, the law was unconstitutional.
- Assessed the law's benefits and burdens, using evidence-based findings that rest on reliable methodology.

While the "undue" standard was clarified, ambiguity remained, and additional battles continued.

Legislators in Texas were quick to respond. Shifting from clinic restrictions, they fashioned a ban on abortions at the first sign of a fetal heartbeat—roughly six weeks of gestation and prior to when many women would know they were pregnant. The "heartbeat law" was hotly debated on both political and medical grounds.[84] Its enforcement was creative. It was fashioned after a *Virginia Law Review* article[85] and several subsequent municipal ordinances. It forbade enforcement by state officials, relying instead on civil suits against abortion providers calling for penalties of $10,000 per abortion. Filers of these suits were soon given the moniker "bounty hunters" by critics of the law. Estimates suggested the law would affect 80%–85% of abortions in Texas. Structured as a civil suit, the law's authors left enforcement in the hands of private individuals and thereby hoped to avoid review of the law in federal courts.[86]

The law, titled The Texas Heartbeat Act, took effect September 1, 2021. The response was immediate. Just over two weeks later, a San Antonio physician published an opinion piece in the *Washington Post,* admitting he had violated the new law.[87] He had done so with the troubling memory of his experience almost a half-century earlier, in 1972, and prior to the *Roe* decision.

As a newly minted physician in the pre-*Roe* period, he had witnessed three teenagers die from illegal abortions. One, he would never forget. The young woman arrived at the emergency room at the hospital where he was working, her vaginal cavity packed with rags to stop the bleeding. She died three days later from organ failure, brought on by a massive infection. For the next 47 years following *Roe,* the physician had been a practicing OB/GYN, delivering some 10,000 babies and providing medical services for women coming to secure his help in abortion clinics where he worked.

He stated, in defiant conclusion,

> Anyone who suspects I have violated the new law can sue me for at least $10,000. They could also sue anybody who helps a person obtain an abortion past the new limit, including, apparently, the driver who brings a patient to my clinic. For me, it is 1972 all over again.

His admission and account were picked up by the national media[88] and a vigorous debate ensued over what was seen at the time as the most restrictive abortion law in the nation.

Less than a day before the law was to take effect, the US Supreme Court, in a single, unsigned paragraph, refused (5-4), on technical grounds, to block the law's implementation. They were not ruling, the Justices noted, on the constitutional standing of the law but questioning the standing of those filing for review. It was a technical argument, but for the time being the law could go into effect.[89] Among opponents, a flurry of furious wonderment followed.[90]

Another law, this time from Mississippi, was waiting in the wings. The law banned abortions after 15 weeks of pregnancy, with exceptions for medical emergencies and fetal abnormalities. Fifteen weeks was approximately two and a half months prior to the point of "viability" established in *Roe.* In that sense, it was in clear violation of almost half a century of Supreme Court rulings. The appeal before the Supreme Court was scheduled for the following December, with a decision anticipated in the summer of 2022. Given recent changes in the composition of the Court, there was widespread speculation that the Court would overturn *Roe,*[91] and many states were ready with "trigger" laws—laws that would go into effect immediately once the Court released its decision.[92] They did not have long to wait.

The Stage Is Set for *Dobbs*

To fully understand the eventual outcome of the case from Mississippi, we need to set the stage. The story begins the year President Obama's second term was ending. In February of that year, Antonin Scalia, a pillar on the Court and a champion of the originalist approach to law, unexpectedly died. Justice Scalia was an icon and had been on the Court 30 years. He was considered one of the most influential Supreme Court Justices of the 20th century and an articulate, outspoken opponent of *Roe v. Wade*.[93] Scalia's supporters were concerned

President Obama would replace him with a liberal Justice, a Justice who saw the Constitution as a living document calling for gradual evolution; a Justice who would, among other issues, support *Roe* and thereby solidify the standing of legal abortion.

For his part, President Obama decided in mid-March to nominate Merrick Garland, the chief judge of the US Court of Appeals, often referred to as the "little Supreme Court." Garland was a widely respected, even admired, judicial moderate who had long been considered a top candidate for Justice of the Supreme Court. In other times, he likely would have been appointed with little opposition. There was one problem—opposition from Scalia's supporters and the conservative wing of the Republican Party.

Most important was the opposition of Senator Mitch McConnell, who was at the time Majority Leader in the Senate. Majority leaders have significant power in setting the Senate agenda and deciding what will, or will not, be considered by senators. With some fanfare, McConnell had announced to an audience in his home state of Kentucky, "One of my proudest moments was when I looked Barack Obama in the eye and I said, 'Mr. President, you will not fill the Supreme Court vacancy.'"[94]

McConnell was true to his promise. He was joined by eleven of his Republican colleagues on the Senate Judiciary Committee, and together they prevented a hearing on the president's nominee. This unprecedented refusal was met with consternation from Garland's supporters, softened a bit by confidence that Hillary Clinton, who had been nominated as her party's candidate for president that July, would win the next presidential election. Still, withholding even a hearing of the president's nomination was as bold as it was infuriating.

Hillary Clinton, as expected, won the popular vote by 2.9 million votes, but Donald J. Trump became president when he carried the Electoral College (304-227). Trump was the fifth president to assume office after losing the popular vote. His ascendency was unanticipated, but it turned out to be determinative when it came to the abortion landscape.

Since Justice Scalia's death and McConnell's refusal to hold hearings on President Obama's nomination, the Supreme Court has been operating with only eight of its nine members. With the presidential election certified and a supportive Senate in place, President Trump lost no time in nominating his choice to fill the ninth seat. Less than two weeks after being sworn in, the Senate received the President's nomination of Neil Gorsuch. Judge Gorsuch was then a sitting judge on the 10th Circuit Court of Appeals and considered a solid conservative addition to the Court. There were some questions about plagiarism, but in early April Gorsuch was confirmed 54-45, largely along contentious party lines. The Supreme Court was back to full strength, with a slight conservative leaning.

A little over a year later, Justice Anthony Kennedy retired from the Court, effective July 31, 2018. Like Antonin Scalia, he had served as Justice for 30 years. Kennedy, a President Reagan appointment, was considered a swing vote who had twice voted to uphold *Roe* in both *Casey* and *Hellerstedt*. The anti-*Roe* camp greeted his retirement with hopeful anticipation. In an interview with National Public Radio, the president of Students for Life noted Kennedy's retirement was

> a day that we've been waiting for. . . . Our goal in the pro-life movement has always been to make abortion illegal and unthinkable. . . . So, we want *Roe* to be overturned . . . and we expect that.[95]

The balance of the Court was shifting further in an anti-*Roe* direction.

On July 9, 2018, a little under a month prior to Justice Kennedy's effective retirement, President Trump nominated Brett Kavanaugh to fill the vacancy. Kavanaugh was a controversial, even provocative, nominee. When nominated in 2003 by President Bush to serve on the US Court of Appeals in Washington, D.C., his confirmation took three years. Opponents launched bitter charges of partisanship for Kavanaugh's vetting of judicial nominations when serving on the White House staff and working prominently drafting what came to be known as the Starr Report recommending the impeachment of President Clinton. The combative three years it took to get his position on the US Court of Appeals in D.C. approved would turn out to be a prelude for the drama about to unfold in the hearings to consider his nomination to the Supreme Court. This time, however, the charge was sexual harassment.

Amidst the dramatic hearings, there were numerous charges and denials of Kavanaugh's drunken sexual harassment of women when he was in high school and college. In total, four charges were made, one eventually withdrawn.[96] Notwithstanding these charges, on October 6, 2018, the Senate, voting again along partisan lines, approved his appointment as Justice, 50-48. Three days later, Kavanaugh assumed full duties on the Supreme Court. The shift toward a Court more favorable to overturning *Roe* was almost complete.

The final step was taken following the death of Ruth Bader Ginsberg. Justice Ginsberg was a champion of women's equality and the right to choose. Known affectionately as the Notorious RBG, movies were made and books written of her life and impact. In recognition of the esteem others held for her, she became the first woman to "lay in state" in the US Capitol following her death. Icon barely captures the admiration and respect she commanded.

Ginsburg's death on September 18, 2020, came in Donald Trump's final year in office. She knew well President Trump was likely to appoint someone deeply at odds with her legal philosophy and had resisted retirement, hoping she could outlive his presidency. Indeed, in a statement dictated to her granddaughter once she knew she would not make it, and perhaps in sarcastic reference to Senator McConnell's blockage of President Obama's nomination of Merrick Garland, she noted, "My most fervent wish is that I will not be replaced until a new president is installed."[97]

Her wish would not be granted. Eight days after Ginsburg's death, President Trump nominated Judge Amy Coney Barrett, then a judge of the US Court of Appeals for the Seventh Circuit, as her replacement. Thirty days later, with modest though vocal opposition, she was confirmed by a Senate vote, again largely along party lines 52-48. With reference to the blocked vote of President Obama's nomination, Senator Schumer, the Senate Minority Leader, underscored the hypocrisy inherent in the vote taken a week before a presidential election. Stating, "After refusing a Democratic nominee to the Supreme Court because an election was eight months away, they will confirm a Republican nominee before an election that is eight days away."[98] On October 27 and 28, 2020, Amy Coney Barrett was sworn in to become the 103rd Associate Justice on the Supreme Court.

Barrett had once clerked for Justice Scalia and frequently described him as her mentor, stating on one occasion, "His judicial philosophy is mine, too." In that sense, she stood in marked contrast to the Justice she was replacing. With this difference noted, like so many others, Justice Barrett held Ruth Bader Ginsburg in high regard. Praising Ginsburg as a trailblazer for women's rights, she noted, "She not only broke glass ceilings; she smashed them."[99]

With sterling legal credentials, a legal philosophy parallel to Antonin Scalia's, the values of a practicing Roman Catholic, and the mother of seven children, Justice Barrett marked a capstone for the transformation of the Supreme Court. The Court, which in 1973 had handed down the 7-2 *Roe v. Wade* decision, had become a court seemingly configured in opposition to *Roe* 6-3 as each of the six conservative justices now on the court had voiced and written in opposition to the landmark decision. There was much speculation that *Roe* would be overturned. It would not take long to test the speculation.

The *Dobbs* Decision

The test came when the Supreme Court agreed in May 2021 to review a case from Mississippi titled *Dobbs v. Jackson Women's Health* Organization. The case involved the only remaining abortion clinic in Mississippi and a new law that prohibited abortion after 15 weeks. The issue the Court agreed to address was whether all pre-viability prohibitions on elective abortions were unconstitutional. Oral arguments focused on both *Roe* and *Casey* and were heard by the Court in December of that year. In a detailed decision, released six months later in June of 2022, Justice Alito wrote for the 6-3 majority:

> We hold that *Roe* and *Casey* must be overruled. The Constitution makes no reference to abortion, and no such right is implicitly protected by any constitutional provision, including the one on which the defenders of *Roe* and *Casey* now chiefly rely—the Due Process Clause of the Fourteenth Amendment.

This answer was greeted with thunderous applause and shouts of "finally" from supporters. It aroused disdain and derision from those opposing. For opposing folks, it was a dark day. The Court's decision was a slap in the face of 50 years of Supreme Court precedent protecting the right to privacy and liberty as applied to abortion and a woman's right to choose.

In his conclusion, Justice Alito wrote:

We end this opinion where we began. Abortion presents a profound moral question. The Constitution does not prohibit the citizens of each state from regulating or prohibiting abortion. *Roe* and *Casey* arrogated that authority. We now overrule those decisions and return that authority to the people and their elected representatives.

On behalf of dissenting Justices, Justice Kagan wrote prophetically for those who disagreed. With a concise objection, she noted:

States will feel free to enact all manner of restrictions. The Mississippi law at issue here bars abortions after the 15th week of pregnancy. Under the majority's ruling, though, another State's law could do so after ten weeks, or five or three or one—or, again, from the moment of fertilization. States have already passed such laws, in anticipation of today's ruling. More will follow.

The Dobbs decision clearly disrupted the abortion landscape. Given the strong tradition and multiplicity of reasons for the Court not overruling decades of its own decisions, what was the rationale for violating the long-standing principle of stare decisis, the Latin phrase meaning "to stand by things decided?" Societies built on law as well as the legitimacy of this Court itself depended upon the predictable stability stare decisis produced. This had long been understood by and was a cornerstone for the Court. Why the reversal? Why overturn decisions released over fifty years ago in *Roe*'s case and 30 years ago for *Casey*?

To begin his argument, Alito pointed to the aforementioned *Yale Law Journal* article written by a respected legal scholar a few months after the *Roe* decision.[100] The Court had gotten it wrong, Alito stated. *Roe* was an "exercise of raw judicial power" and had "sparked a national controversy that has embittered our political culture for a half century." This power, Alito continued, was not anchored in the liberty or privacy implications of the 14th or any other Amendment in the Constitution. The decision on whether to prohibit or permit abortion should be returned to the states. They were wrong to have taken it away.

The Court, however, was not unanimous. Justice Roberts, the sitting Chief Justice, was supportive of the basic decision but voiced concerns and reportedly lobbied his colleagues to moderate their positions.[101] Referring to the three cases the Court used to set aside stare decisis, he noted differences with this case:

The opinion in *Brown* [ruled racial segregation of children in public schools was unconstitutional] was unanimous and eleven pages long; this one is neither. *Barnette* [students possess some level of First Amendment rights and a compulsory flag salute in public schools was invalidated] was decided only three years after the decision it overruled, three Justices having had second thoughts. And *West Coast Hotel* [establishing minimum wages for women was constitutional] was issued against a backdrop of unprecedented economic despair [the Great Depression] that focused attention on the fundamental flaws of existing precedent. It also was part of a sea change in this Court's interpretation of the Constitution, "signaling the demise of an entire line of important precedents," a feature the Court expressly disclaims in today's decision. None of these leading cases, in short, provides a template for what the Court does today.

The Chief Justice advocated a more measured approach, not overturning *Roe* and *Casey* in total but focusing on what he saw as the questionable point of "viability" they had put in place. Indeed, Roberts wrote, this is what Mississippi had asked for:

> In urging our review, Mississippi stated that its case was "an ideal vehicle" to "reconsider the bright-line viability rule," and that a judgment in its favor would "not require the Court to overturn" *Roe v. Wade,* and *Planned Parenthood of Southeastern Pa. v. Casey.* Today, the Court nonetheless rules for Mississippi by doing just that. I would take a more measured course. I agree with the Court that the viability line established by *Roe* and *Casey* should be discarded.

Later, in his opinion, the Chief Justice continued:

> Here, there is a clear path to deciding this case correctly without overruling *Roe* all the way down to the studs: recognize that the viability line must be discarded, as the majority rightly does, and leave for another day whether to reject any right to an abortion at all.

Chief Justice Roberts was urging action with a narrower scope than the one being taken. Still, he understood all issues would not be resolved and follow-on questions would come to the Court:

> I am not sure, for example, that a ban on terminating a pregnancy from the moment of conception must be treated the same under the Constitution as a ban after fifteen weeks. A thoughtful Member of this Court once counseled that the difficulty of a question "admonishes us to observe the wise limitations on our function and to confine ourselves to deciding only what is necessary to the disposition of the immediate case."

The Chief Justice understood well that states would one day have to establish "a bright line that clearly distinguishes abortion and infanticide." Was it when a fetal heartbeat was detected, when the fetus could experience pain, at the moment of conception, or some other point? For Roberts, these were questions for another day.

Speaking for her judicial colleagues opposing the decision, Justice Kagan gave voice to even stronger concerns. Noting the folly of not recognizing the Constitution's protection of liberty and privacy in the context of abortion and the wisdom of the balance achieved when the Court drew the line of "viability" and thereby considered both the life of the mother and the life of the fetus, she wrote:

> Today, the Court discards that balance. It says that from the very moment of fertilization, a woman has no rights to speak of. A State can force her to bring a pregnancy to term, even at the steepest personal and familial costs. An abortion restriction, the majority holds, is permissible whenever rational, the lowest level of scrutiny known to the law. And because, as the Court has often stated, protecting fetal life is rational, some states have enacted laws extending to all forms of abortion procedure, including taking medication in one's own home.

Justice Kagan continued, raising the crescendo:

> They have passed laws without any exceptions for when the woman is the victim of rape or incest. Under those laws, a woman will have to bear her rapist's child or a young girl her father's—no matter if doing so will destroy her life. So too, after today's ruling, some states may compel women to carry to term a fetus with severe physical anomalies—for example, one afflicted with Tay-Sachs disease, sure to die within a few years of birth. States may even argue that a prohibition on abortion need make no provision for protecting a woman from risk of death or physical harm.

Justice Kagan was not finished. She turned next to how the now permitted laws would be enforced.

> Enforcement of all these draconian restrictions will also be left largely to the states' devices. A State can of course impose criminal penalties on abortion providers, including lengthy prison sentences. But some states will not stop there. Perhaps, in the wake of today's decision, a state law will criminalize the woman's conduct too, incarcerating or fining her for daring to seek or obtain an abortion. And as Texas has recently shown, a state can turn neighbor against neighbor, enlisting fellow citizens in the effort to root out anyone who tries to get an abortion, or to assist another in doing so.

· How did the Court get to this point? For Justice Kagan, it was because they had abandoned core values:

> *Roe* and *Casey* were from the beginning, and are even more now, embedded in core constitutional concepts of individual freedom, and of the equal rights of citizens to decide on the shape of their lives. Those legal concepts, one might even say, have gone far toward defining what it means to be an American. For in this Nation, we do not believe that a government controlling all private choices is compatible with a free people. So, we do not (as the majority insists today) place everything within "the reach of majorities and [government] officials."

Kagan warned that abandoning these principles would have far-reaching consequences:

> And no one should be confident that this majority is done with its work. The right *Roe* and *Casey* recognized does not stand alone. To the contrary, the Court has linked it for decades to other settled freedoms involving bodily integrity, familial relationships, and procreation. Most obviously, the right to terminate a pregnancy arose straight out of the right to purchase and use contraception.

Dobbs abandoned the 14th Amendment's applicability to liberty and privacy as applied to abortion. Perhaps having in mind the Supreme Court's widely quoted statement in *Eisenstadt v. Baird*,

> If the right of privacy means anything, it is the right of the individual, married or single, to be free from unwarranted governmental intrusion into matters so fundamentally affecting a person as the decision whether to bear or beget a child,

Justice Kagan speculated about the broader implications of *Dobbs*.

> Consider, as our last word on this issue, contraception. The Constitution, of course, does not mention that word. And there is no historical right to contraception, of the kind the majority insists on. To the contrary, the American legal landscape in the decades after the Civil War was littered with bans on the sale of contraceptive devices.

Justice Kagan wrote further to hammer her concerns home.

> The right Roe and Casey recognized does not stand alone. To the contrary, the Court has linked it for decades to other settled freedoms involving bodily integrity, familial relationships, and procreation. Most obviously, the right to

terminate a pregnancy arose straight out of the right to purchase and use contraception. . . . In turn, those rights led, more recently, to rights of same-sex
intimacy and marriage.

In fact, Justice Thomas, who had voted with the majority in *Dobbs*, urged in his
concurring addendum that the Court reopen attention given the very thing that
worried Kagan and her dissenting colleagues. Namely, that further consideration
of cases involving use of contraception, same-sex relations, and same-sex marriage was called for.

Clearly, the post-*Dobbs* landscape was littered with unanswered questions.
Justice Alito wrote of the road ahead:

> We do not pretend to know how our political system or society will respond
> to today's decision overruling *Roe* and *Casey*. And even if we could foresee
> what will happen, we would have no authority to let that knowledge influence
> our decision. We can only do our job, which is to interpret the law, apply long-
> standing principles of *stare decisis*, and decide this case accordingly.

How would the states respond? How did *Dobbs* affect the right to privacy and
liberty more generally? It was and remains an uncertain future.

States Respond

As the case from Mississippi wound its way through the appellate system and
on to the Supreme Court and the eventual *Dobbs v. Jackson Women's Health
Organization* decision, there was widespread anticipation that *Roe* would be
overturned. As already noted, many states had laws waiting in the wings.[102]
These laws came to be known as "trigger laws," set to go into effect when the
anticipated overturning of *Roe* was final. It worked. Almost immediately following the decision, media outlets carried stories of new abortion bans taking hold
in numerous states.

The *Dobbs* decision was released in late June. Three months later, in late September, 13 states had enacted laws that prohibited abortion at any stage of pregnancy, some granting exceptions for the pregnant woman's life or if pregnancy
had resulted from rape or incest. Many of these laws were challenged in court. A
year later, the picture began to clarify.

In August 2023, the *Journal of the American Medical Association* (*JAMA*)
carried an article noting the "Vast Changes to the Abortion Landscape."[103]
JAMA estimated 14 states had banned abortion. It was widely predicted that this
would soon rise to 24 states. Seven of the newly passed laws established cutoff points ranging from 6 to 18 weeks, generally linked to a detected heartbeat
or the assertion of fetal suffering. Some of these laws carried what seemed to
many opponents as draconian provisions: penalties ranging from one year to life

imprisonment and fines up to $100,000. In Arkansas, for example, the law read: "Performing or attempting to perform an abortion is an unclassified felony with a fine not to exceed one hundred thousand dollars ($100,000) or imprisonment not to exceed ten (10) years, or both."

Just west of Arkansas, Oklahoma's governor signed a law banning abortion following conception, thus becoming the strictest law in the nation. Taking the lead from its neighbor, Texas, the Oklahoma law was to be enforced by civil lawsuit rather than criminal prosecution. Oklahoma's governor released a statement, saying:

> From the moment life begins at conception is when we have a responsibility as human beings to do everything we can to protect that baby's life and the life of the mother. That is what I believe and that is what the majority of Oklahomans believe.

For their part, Oklahoma's abortion providers planned to stop providing services as soon as the law was signed.[104]

In contrast, as the year passed following the release of *Dobbs,* a multiplicity of states launched or affirmed laws protecting the right to abortion.[105] In California, Michigan, and Vermont, there were ballot measures enshrining the right to choose an abortion in the states' constitutions. By May 2023, Montana had reaffirmed the existing state constitutional protection for "procreative autonomy" and had struck down a state law barring registered nurses from performing abortions. In other states, there was increased funding for abortion clinics and requirements for insurance companies to cover procedures and protections for individuals providing or seeking abortions.

In addition, there were lawsuits in numerous states challenging existing restrictive abortion laws.[106] Overall, it was a mixed picture as State laws evolved. In overview, post-*Dobbs* abortion bills banned abortion at the following stages after conception: upon detection of a "heartbeat," when the fetus feels pain, or when viability is achieved.[107]

In most states, though not all, exceptions were made for the mother's life, lethal fetal anomalies, and whether the pregnancy was the result of rape, incest, or other felonious intercourse.[108]

The Reality of "Exceptions" in Total Ban States:
The Case of Kate Cox in Texas

Texas is one of the most prohibitive states in the nation when it comes to abortion. Though its three overlapping laws do not hold people who receive abortions criminally responsible, they do punish anyone who might help, including the physicians who provide abortions or those who provide any form of aid to a person in securing an abortion (e.g., an Uber driver). Similar to other restrictive states, Texas allows for exceptions to save the life or prevent "substantial impairment of major bodily function" of a pregnant patient, but it does not make an exception for lethal fetal abnormalities. Pregnant women are expected to carry these pregnancies to term even if there is a high probability that the patient will miscarry or if there is little hope for the child to survive once born.

In reality, the health of the pregnant person and that of the fetus are often interconnected. This was the case for Kate Cox, a Texas mother of two. Her fetus was diagnosed with trisomy 18, a genetic anomaly that usually ends in miscarriage, stillbirth, or infant death, and that frequently causes severe physical pain and impairment of future fertility for the mother. The earliest this diagnosis can be made is about ten weeks—four weeks after one of Texas' three abortion bans.

Following four visits in two weeks for emergency care related to her pregnancy, Cox' physicians recommended an abortion to protect her ability to get pregnant again in the future. Given the legal precariousness of performing abortions in the state, her physicians wished to ensure they were protected from prosecution before performing the abortion—they sought, and were given approval, from a Dallas district judge. Soon after, Texas Attorney General Ken Paxton asked the Texas Supreme Court to intervene. Rather than wait to hear of the court's decision, the now 20-week-pregnant Cox obtained her abortion in another state. There was little surprise when the nine justices eventually released their decision—they'd sided with Paxton, determined that a physician's "good-faith belief" did not meet the legal standard of "reasonable medical judgment" (though neither term is defined in Texas law) and that Cox's case didn't meet the medical exception.[109]

It is an evolving picture, as some states continued to craft their laws and others awaited court decisions.

Current Legal Status of Abortion in US States

After *Dobbs*, states have sought to clarify their positions on abortions in two ways: through interpretations of state constitutions or through implementation of pre-existing or new legislation.

Every state has its own unique constitution. Post-*Dobbs*, these constitutions have become important battlegrounds for abortion rights. Numerous court decisions have clarified whether or not state constitutions protect the right to abortion.

Fourteen state courts have recognized that their constitutions protect at least some level of abortion rights (e.g., saving of a person's life), though in two of these cases (West Virginia and Tennessee), voters later approved ballot initiatives that rejected these constitutional protections. Three states have denied that their constitutions protect abortion rights (Idaho, Iowa, and South Carolina). Other states have yet to consider abortion restrictions in light of the state's constitution.[110]

Most states have clarified their positions on abortion through legislation, often based on some consideration of GA or fetal development.[111] Currently, states' abortion bans based on fetal development or GA exist on a continuum, from total bans to unrestricted access. To be clear, however, even the most restrictive "total ban" states may allow for an abortion under some exceptions, such as pregnancies that are the result of rape or incest, to protect the life or health of the pregnant person, or in cases with severe fetal anomalies. In Oklahoma, for example, an abortion may be legal in order to "save the life of a pregnant patient in a medical emergency." In these limited cases, Oklahoma even allows for Medicaid or private health insurance to be used to pay for the abortion. However, Oklahoma makes no exceptions for pregnancies that are the result of rape or incest. In five "total ban" states, exceptions are made for rape-related pregnancies, but often survivors are required to report their rape to law enforcement before being allowed to undergo the procedure. This is a significant hurdle, as rape survivors are some of the least likely of victims to report to the police—only about one in five report.[112] Finally, only six of the "total ban" states make exceptions for incest.[113]

The current legal status of abortion in the states:

Full Abortion Bans (14 states): Alabama, Arkansas, Idaho, Indiana, Kentucky, Louisiana, Mississippi, Missouri, North Dakota, Oklahoma, South Dakota, Tennessee, Texas, and West Virginia. It is estimated that half of states will ban or almost ban all abortions.[114]

"Heartbeat" Bans (all abortion procedures are banned after fetal cardiac activity can be detected, about six weeks of gestation; four states): Florida, Georgia, Ohio, and South Carolina.

Pre-viability Bans (early abortions are banned prior to fetal viability, 7 states): Arizona (15 weeks), Iowa (22 weeks), Kansas (22 weeks), Nebraska (12 weeks), North Carolina (12 weeks), Utah (18 weeks), and Wisconsin (22 weeks).

Viability Bans (abortions are banned after fetal viability, about 24 weeks of gestation; 17 states): California, Connecticut, Delaware, Hawaii, Illinois, Maine, Massachusetts, Michigan, Montana, Nevada, New Hampshire, New York, Pennsylvania, Rhode Island, Virginia (third trimester), Washington, and Wyoming.

Unrestricted Access (not restricted based on GA; nine states/jurisdictions): Alaska, Colorado, Maryland, Minnesota, New Jersey, New Mexico, Oregon, Vermont, and Washington, D.C.

Public Opinion on Abortion Post-*Dobbs*

As the year following *Dobbs* came to an end, the Gallup polling agency asked a national sample a four-part question about where they stood on the question of abortion[115]:

Do you think abortions should be legal under any circumstances, legal only under certain circumstances or illegal in all circumstances? (If legal only under certain circumstances): Do you think abortion should be legal in most circumstances or only in a few circumstances?

Responses were wide ranging: legal under any circumstance −34%; legal under most circumstances −13%; legal in only a few circumstances −36%; illegal in all circumstances −13%; no opinion 3%. When these responses were compared to the geographic distribution of and demographic support for laws passed, there was a close fit to what was noted earlier: most resistance to abortion was concentrated in the southern and southwestern US.[116]

Questions to Be Answered

Clearly, the Dobbs decision was a jolt to the legal system. It had long been believed, as the Supreme Court had stated in 1891, "No right is held more sacred, or is more carefully guarded, by the common law, than the right of every individual to the possession and control of his own person, free from all restraint or interference of others."[117]

Then again, almost four decades later, the Court noted:

The makers of our Constitution undertook to secure conditions favorable to the pursuit of happiness. . . . They conferred, as against the government, the right to be let alone—the most comprehensive of rights and the right most valued by civilized men. To protect that right, every unjustifiable intrusion by the government upon the privacy of the individual, whatever the means employed, must be deemed a violation of the Fourth Amendment.[118]

Building on these principles, the Court, 15 years later, invalidated an Oklahoma law providing for the sterilization of certain criminals, ruling it violated the equal protection clause of the Fourteenth Amendment. Stating that procreation is a fundamental right, the Court wrote:

We are dealing here with legislation which involves one of the basic civil rights of man. Marriage and procreation are fundamental to the very existence and survival of the race. The power to sterilize, if exercised, may have subtle, far-reaching and devastating effects. In evil or reckless hands it can cause races or types which are inimical to the dominant group to wither and disappear. There is no redemption for the individual whom the law touches.[119]

Keeping the trend alive, in 1965, the Court underscored the importance of "penumbral" implications embedded in general constitutional principles in a case from Connecticut involving contraception and, as it turned out, directly tied to *Dobbs:*

> The right of association contained in the penumbra of the First Amendment is one, as we have seen. The Third Amendment, in its prohibition against the quartering of soldiers "in any house" in time of peace without the consent of the owner, is another facet of that privacy. The Fourth Amendment explicitly affirms the "right of the people to be secure in their persons, houses, papers, and effects, against unreasonable searches and seizures." The Fifth Amendment, in its Self-Incrimination Clause, enables the citizen to create a zone of privacy which government may not force him to surrender to his detriment. The Ninth Amendment provides: "The enumeration in the Constitution, of certain rights, shall not be construed to deny or disparage others retained by the people."

Two years later, the Court held in *Loving v. Virginia*, involving a law prohibiting interracial marriage:

> These statutes also deprive the Lovings of liberty without due process of law in violation of the Due Process Clause of the Fourteenth Amendment. The freedom to marry has long been recognized as one of the vital personal rights essential to the orderly pursuit of happiness by free men.[120]

The stage was set for the right to privacy in *Roe*. Importantly, the Court found:

> The Constitution does not explicitly mention any right of privacy. In a line of decisions, however, going back perhaps as far as *Union Pacific R. Co. v. Botsford*, 141 U.S. 250, 251 (1891), the Court has recognized that a right of personal privacy, or a guarantee of certain areas or zones of privacy, does exist under the Constitution.[121]

Again, in *Casey,* the Court wrote:

> The woman's constitutional liberty interest also involves her freedom to decide matters of the highest privacy and the most personal nature. Cf. *Whalen v. Roe,* 429 U. S. 589, 598–600 (1977).[122]

Contrary to the principle and practice of stare decisis, *Dobbs* found abortion an exception:

> As to precedent, citing a broad array of cases, the Court found support for a constitutional "right of personal privacy." But Roe conflated the right to shield information from disclosure and the right to make and implement important personal decisions without governmental interference.

Using this distinction between disclosure and decision-making, the *Dobbs* Court overruled both *Roe* and *Casey.* They seemed to be saying the right to privacy that is supported by the Constitution is limited to the ability to keep personal information private and does not extend to the ability to make decisions about one's affairs (e.g., abortion) without government intervention. When it came to abortion, privacy and liberty were not constitutionally protected. These frequently fought over Supreme Court decisions, *Roe* and *Casey*, were overruled. It was a new day, a long-awaited ray of sunshine for supporters. The new day was clouded, cold, and dreary for those in opposition. As stated in the dissenting opinion, "The Constitution will, today's majority holds, provide no shield, despite its guarantees of liberty and equality for all."

The Coming Years

As reactions to *Dobbs* came forward, questions arose regarding its broader implications. They came in earliest form when Justice Kagan wrote of troublesome loose ends for her and Court colleagues dissenting from the *Dobbs* decision:

> Must a state law allow abortions when necessary to protect a woman's life and health? And if so, exactly when? How much risk to a woman's life can a state force her to incur, before the Fourteenth Amendment's protection of life kicks in? Suppose a patient with pulmonary hypertension has a 30-to-50 percent risk of dying with ongoing pregnancy; is that enough? And short of death, how much illness or injury can the State require her to accept, consistent with the Amendment's protection of liberty and equality? Further, the Court may face questions about the application of abortion regulations to medical care most people view as quite different from abortion. What about the morning-after pill? IUDs? In vitro fertilization?

The questions were many, the answers few.

Justice Kagan was not alone. During the year following *Dobbs*, several issues of Dobbs' uncertain impact were noted. Where did the use of assisted reproductive technologies (ART) such as IVF, as well as medications used to terminate early pregnancy, stand?

By the time *Dobbs* was decided, the use of mifepristone and misoprostol to terminate pregnancy had become common practice. Both drugs were considered safe and had been approved by the FDA. In the same 2023 JAMA article referred to above, the authors concluded, "The FDA's decision was supported by evidence that mifepristone successfully terminates pregnancy in more than 99% of cases, with extremely low risks of major complications." By early 2022, these medications were used in slightly over half of pregnancy terminations nationwide.[123]

Whether to prohibit, regulate, or simply take a hands-off position became the question. Perhaps the most salient unanswered issue had to do with the acquisition and use of medications to terminate the pregnancy during early gestation. Levonorgestrel was available without a prescription; ulipristal acetate was available, but only with a prescription. Two additional safe and highly effective medications: mifepristone, followed by misoprostol up to 48 hours later, would end a pregnancy through ten weeks gestation 92%–99% of the time.[124]

Could states block the purchase and use of these medications? Such medications seemed to be protected given the privacy rulings declaring unconstitutional the Connecticut and Massachusetts contraception laws directly preceding *Roe*. Given the step away from constitutionally protected privacy in Dobbs and the postconception utility of some drugs, however, there was uncertainty. Indeed, in August 2023 the Supreme Court agreed to hear a case from Texas calling for restrictions on the medications.[125]

Also, looming was the question of IVF and other ART. IVF is a procedure used to assist procreation by fertilizing an ovum outside the body and then introducing the conceptus into a woman's body for gestation. When the first successful IVF baby was born four and a half decades earlier in 1978, there had been much controversy. IVF seemed unnatural to many. Were we playing God? Would the baby be born with abnormalities?

Since the first successful IVF birth of Louise Brown (who became a parent herself in 2006), however, the procedure has become widely used, with an estimated 12 million plus births taking place globally.[126] Still, questions remain. Given the nature of IVF procedures, often more embryos are created than used. Along with the embryo(s) introduced into the woman's womb, some are frozen, some discarded, some donated to other families with infertility problems, and still others used in such projects as stem-cell research. For those believing protected human life begins at conception, this presents a problem. The answers are evolving.

Many of the swirling issues were brought to the fore a year and a half after the *Dobbs* decision, in February 2024, when the Alabama Supreme Court held that under state law, frozen embryos are people. Shock, anger, and confusion from citizens and prospective parents seeking conception assistance emerged instantly. There was also praise from those who believed the Court's action reflected God's will. Podcasts were aired, and numerous articles published.[127]

In its decision declaring microscopic frozen embryos as people, the Alabama Supreme Court supported its reasoning with religion-laced rhetoric:

> We believe that each human being from the moment of conception is made in the image of God, created by Him to reflect His likeness. It is as if the People of Alabama took what was spoken of the prophet Jeremiah and applied it to every unborn person in the state.

This ruling clearly put citizens seeking IVF assistance in Alabama in a quandary. IVF was pro-life. Declaring frozen embryos as people puts restraints on this life-enhancing possibility.

The broader legal standing of IVF is evolving. A year after *Dobbs,* there were no laws banning IVF, but if a state defines the conceptus as the beginning of protected life, there will be questions to ask. As with early-term abortion-inducing medications, with IVF in the post-*Dobbs* era, we are entering an uncertain future.

Another general issue: Given *Dobbs*, what is the general legal standing of "privacy?" Just short of a year following the decision, the American Bar Association published an article stating,

> *Dobbs* could have significant and unanticipated implications for the law of privacy and the law of free expression . . . the Court in *Dobbs* could unsettle a number of important privacy and free speech principles that we have come to think of as established.

By setting aside the Court's long-standing commitment to stare decisis, the article continued, "Everything we think we know about the Constitution seems up for grabs and may be."[128]

As we have seen, the Court gave justifications for abandoning its adherence to their preceding decisions by noting that the *Roe* and *Casey* decisions had "conflated the right to shield information from disclosure and the right to make and implement important personal decisions without governmental interference." The first remains in place. In the case of abortion, the latter has been abandoned.

What about choosing a marital partner? This would seem to fall into the category of implementing personal decisions. The standing of inter-racial and same-sex marriage has been declared constitutionally protected. These Supreme Court decisions were grounded in the due process clause of the Fourteenth Amendment. Yet, noting the idea that the *Roe* Court conflated the right to shield information with the right to implement important personal decisions, the constitutional ties between the Fourteenth Amendment and abortion were cut. Why is the same rationale not applicable to the choice and implementation of marital decisions? Justice Kagan, writing for the minority dissenting in *Dobbs,* worried that it might be.

What about the right to privacy in the rapidly developing area of information tracking? A person's movements can now be thoroughly tracked. This becomes increasingly important as states implement abortion banning bills with accompanying sanctions and increasingly rely on civil suits by individual citizens for enforcement. For example, GPS tracking can now routinely map visits to abortion clinics. This information can be accessed at low cost and used by law enforcement officials and citizens alike. Can we block governmental access? It would seem so, given the current Supreme Court's stance on "disclosure" of information. Yet, with probable cause that something illegal has occurred, data can be gathered by government officials. Why does the same logic not apply to abortion? What about blockage of private citizen access to tracking information in states that rely on civil suits to enforce abortion laws? Both open questions.

Concerns over these and related issues emerged just after the *Dobbs* decision was released. An article worrying over the questions embedded in rapidly evolving information technology, written three months after *Dobbs*, stated, "*Dobbs* has drastically altered how judges, lawmakers, and juries are going to view privacy. The value of our privacy is clear and the harms that come from violating it are easy to see."[129]

We end with what is in many ways the most perplexing question about the future: With Dobbs now the law of the land, will we see a return to the pre-*Roe* maternal mortality levels and medical costs associated with illegal abortions? Again, there are no easy answers, but many reasons for concern. In October 2022, three months after the release of Dobbs, the National Library of Medicine published a study titled, "The Medical and Financial Burden of Illegal Abortion." Carefully reviewing the existing literature, the article highlighted "the known effects and medical complications of illegal abortion and the financial impact of the procedure's legal status."[130] The findings painted a daunting, sometimes brutal, picture.

Among those seeking illegal abortions in non-professional settings, many desperate means were used in the pre-*Roe* years. These included, the researchers noted, "foreign bodies placed in the uterus through the cervix, such as sticks dipped in oil, wire, knitting needles, coat hangers, ballpoint pens, and air blown in by either a syringe or turkey baster." In addition, "Self-medication with toxic chemicals such as turpentine, bleach, detergent solutions, quinine, and strong teas" were employed. The results were frequently fatal. Citing the World Health Organization, the authors noted, "The main causes of death from unsafe abortion are hemorrhage, infection, sepsis, genital trauma, and necrotic bowel."

In the years preceding *Roe,* the article continued, "Complications of unsafe, illegal abortions were common occurrences in medical wards, and the healthcare system was taxed with treating these preventable situations." Facing medical emergencies precipitated by illegal abortions, physicians, nurses, medical procedures, and facilities were activated. The cost, the researchers estimated using then current data, would approach $6.4 billion per year. Clearly, we are dealing with financially demanding conditions, conditions that differentially impact those without insurance and those with access to few economic means.

Illegal Abortion

An illegal abortion is typically defined as an abortion procedure performed by a nonphysician.[131] Though most women with unwanted pregnancies carry their pregnancies to term when abortion is illegal, it remains clear that some women will still obtain them. The problem is, of course, when done in unregulated secret, abortion can become dangerous and even life-threatening. According to one study, the risks of death for an illegal abortion are approximately eight times greater than the risks for a legal abortion. These risks are most pronounced for poor women (who have fewer resources to pay for the procedure) and those who live in rural locations, far from hospitals that can treat them for botched illegal abortions.[132]

Because of their illegality, accurate statistics on the number of illegal abortions are difficult to come by. Some researchers have derived estimates of the number of illegal abortions based on occurrences that can be more easily measured: the number of hospitalizations and deaths that have resulted from illegal abortions. These numbers are obtained from local surveys and, beginning in 1972, from the Center for Disease Control's national data on abortion-related mortality. In 1955, an expert panel estimated between 200,000 and 1.2 million illegal abortions occurred in the United States annually. Estimates calculated shortly after the *Roe* decision suggest that the annual number of illegal abortions in the United States was about 17,000 by 1974.

Even when abortion is legal, some women still seek illegal abortions. Depending on the survey, between 1% and 5% of women report having tried to end a pregnancy on their own, typically using herbs, prescription drugs, or other substances.[133]

Faced with these financially demanding, frequently fatal medical conditions, there are reasons to worry about the coming years. The Commonwealth Fund has published a study titled, "The U.S. Maternal Health Divide: The Limited Maternal Health Services and Worse Outcomes of States Proposing New Abortion Restrictions."[134] In this detailed, carefully crafted study, the authors conclude: "(F)or every major racial or ethnic group, maternal death rates are higher in abortion-restriction states compared to abortion-access states." It is a finding replicated numerous times by other researchers.[135] The hopeful news is that the availability of pregnancy-terminating medications in the post-*Dobbs* years is clearly greater than in the pre-*Roe* years. No doubt this will influence mortality and medical costs among those seeking to terminate their pregnancies. Even with these now available medications, however, it remains an open, highly troubling question.

One thing is clear. The case from Mississippi, *Dobbs v. Jackson Women's Health Organization,* has had a seismic effect on the abortion terrain in the United States. No doubt about this. We close where we began. Many outcomes remain uncertain, but two points are clear: (1) Resolution of the embedded moral dilemmas will be driven by differential empathy, and (2) tension will remain.

Notes

1 Nate Cohn, "Do Americans Support Abortion Rights? Depends on the State," *The New York Times*, May 4, 2022, www.nytimes.com/2022/05/04/upshot/polling-abortion-states.html; Hannah Hartig, "About Six-in-Ten Americans Say Abortion Should Be Legal in All or Most Cases," June, 13, 2022, www.pewresearch.org/fact-tank/2022/06/13/about-six-in-ten-americans-say-abortion-should-be-legal-in-all-or-most-cases-2/.
2 Lydia Saad, "Broader Support for Abortion Rights Continues Post-Dobbs," *Gallup*, June 14, 2023, https://news.gallup.com/poll/506759/broader-support-abortion-rights-continues-post-dobbs.aspx; Besheer Mohamed, Hannah Hartig, Anna Schiller, and Kelsey Beveridge, "America's Abortion Quandary," *Pew Research Center*, May 6, 2022, www.pewresearch.org/religion/2022/05/06/americas-abortion-quandary/.
3 Lydia Saad, "Broader Support for Abortion Rights Continues Post-Dobbs," *Gallup*, June 14, 2023, https://news.gallup.com/poll/506759/broader-support-abortion-rights-continues-post-dobbs.aspx; Besheer Mohamed, Hannah Hartig, Anna Schiller and Kelsey Beveridge, "America's Abortion Quandary," *Pew Research Center*, May 6, 2022, www.pewresearch.org/religion/2022/05/06/americas-abortion-quandary/.
4 Rachel Jones et al., "Long-Term Decline in US Abortions Reverses, Showing Rising Need for Abortion as Supreme Court Is Poised to Overturn Roe v. Wade," January 1, 2022, www.guttmacher.org/article/2022/06/long-term-decline-us-abortions-reverses-showing-rising-need-abortion-supreme-court.
5 Katherine Kortsmit et al., "Abortion Surveillance—United States, 2020," *Surveillance Summaries* 71, no 10 (November 25, 2022): 1–27, www.cdc.gov/mmwr/volumes/71/ss/ss7110a1.htm; Rachel Jones et al., "Medication Abortion Now Accounts for More Than Half of All US Abortions," February 2022, www.guttmacher.org/article/2022/02/medication-abortion-now-accounts-more-half-all-us-abortions.
6 Jenna Jerman, Rachel Jones, and Tsuyoshi Onda, "Characteristics of U.S. Abortion Patients in 2014 and Changes Since 2008," May 2016, www.guttmacher.org/report/characteristics-us-abortion-patients-2014.
7 M. Antonia Biggs, Heather Gould, and Diana Greene Foster, "Understanding Why Women Seek Abortions in the U.S.," *BMC Women's Health* 13, no. 1 (2013): 1–13; Lawrence B. Finer, Lori F. Frohwirth, Lindsay A. Dauphinee, Susheela Singh, and Ann M. Moore, "Reasons U.S. Women Have Abortions: Quantitative and Qualitative Perspectives," September 2005, www.guttmacher.org/journals/psrh/2005/reasons-us-women-have-abortions-quantitative-and-qualitative-perspectives.
8 Malcolm Potts and Martha Campbell, "History of Contraception," *Gynecology and Obstetrics* 6, no. 8 (2002): 1–23.

9   Malcolm Potts and Martha Campbell, "History of Contraception," *Gynecology and Obstetrics* 6, no. 8 (2002): 1–23.
10   Malcolm Potts and Martha Campbell, "History of Contraception," *Gynecology and Obstetrics* 6, no. 8 (2002): 1–23.
11   Pope Paul VI, "On the Regulation of Birth," *Humanae Vitae, Encyclical Letter*, July 25, 1968.
12   Malcolm Potts and Martha Campbell, "History of Contraception," *Gynecology and Obstetrics* 6, no. 8 (2002): 1–23.
13   John Rock, *The Time Has Come: A Catholic Doctor's Proposals to End the Battle Over Birth Control*. New York: Avon Books, 1963; Malcolm Gladwell, "What the Co-Inventor of the Pill Didn't Know: Menstruation Can Endanger Women's Health," March 5, 2000, www.newyorker.com/magazine/2000/03/13/john-rocks-error.
14   Malcolm Potts and Martha Campbell, "History of Contraception," *Gynecology and Obstetrics* 6, no. 8 (2002): 1–23.
15   Christopher Ingraham, "Charted: The Religions that Make the Most Babies," *The Washington Post*, May 12, 2015, www.washingtonpost.com/news/wonk/wp/2015/05/12/charted-the-religions-that-make-the-most-babies/; Lyman Stone, "America's Growing Religious-Secular Fertility Divide," *Institute for Family Studies*, August 8, 2022, https://ifstudies.org/blog/americas-growing-religious-secular-fertility-divide.
16   Patrick T. Brown, "Catholics Are Just as Likely to Get an Abortion as Other U.S. Women. Why?" *American Magazine*, January 24, 2018, www.americamagazine.org/politics-society/2018/01/24/catholics-are-just-likely-get-abortion-other-us-women-why.
17   Don Colburn, "Abortion Rates Vary," *The Washington Post*, October 11, 1988, www.washingtonpost.com/archive/lifestyle/wellness/1988/10/11/abortion-rates-vary/4948caec-ec72-4028-b4d0-cd2e6873a73a/.
18   *Griswold v. Connecticut*, 381 U.S. 479, 1965.
19   Malcolm Potts and Martha Campbell, "History of Contraception," *Gynecology and Obstetrics* 6, no. 8 (2002): 1–23.
20   Abraham Stone, "Social and Legal Status of Contraception, The-Part I," *North Carolina Law Review* 22, no. 3 (1944): 212.
21   Malcolm Potts and Martha Campbell, "History of Contraception," *Gynecology and Obstetrics* 6, no. 8 (2002): 1–23.
22   Malcolm Potts and Martha Campbell, "History of Contraception," *Gynecology and Obstetrics* 6, no. 8 (2002): 1–23.
23   Mary Zeigler, "Eugenic Feminism: Mental Hygiene, the Women's Movement, and the Campaign for Eugenic Legal Reform, 1900–1935," *Harvard Journal of Law and Gender* 31 (2008): 211.
24   Mary Zeigler, "Eugenic Feminism: Mental Hygiene, the Women's Movement, and the Campaign for Eugenic Legal Reform, 1900–1935," *Harvard Journal of Law and Gender* 31 (2008): 211.
25   Amita Kelly, "Fact Check: Was Planned Parenthood Started to 'Control' The Black Population?" *NPR*, August 14, 2015, www.npr.org/sections/itsallpolitics/2015/08/14/432080520/fact-check-was-planned-parenthood-started-to-control-the-black-population.
26   Kristin Luker, *Abortion and the Politics of Motherhood*. Berkeley, CA: University of California Press, 1984, 62–65.
27   Sherri Chessen, "Rich Little Poor Girl: Sherri's Story Was Told in the Sissy Spacek Movie, 'A Private Matter'," www.veteranfeministsofamerica.org/legacy/Sherri%20Chessen.htm.

28 Carole E. Joffe, Tracy A. Weitz and Clare L. Stacey, "Uneasy Allies: Pro-choice Physicians, Feminist Health Activists and the Struggle for Abortion Rights," *Sociology of Health & Illness* 26, no. 6 (2004): 775–796.

29 Caelyn Pender, "'San Francisco Nine': The Case that Prompted California's Expansion of Abortion Laws," *KRON4*, July 24, 2022, www.kron4.com/news/san-francisco-nine-the-case-that-prompted-californias-expansion-of-abortion-laws/.

30 Sheldon Ekland-Olson, *Who Lives, Who Dies, Who Decides?*, 3rd ed. New York: Routledge, 2018, 135–142.

31 Kristin Luker, *Abortion and the Politics of Motherhood*. Berkeley, CA: University of California Press, 1984, 97.

32 Sherri Chessen, "Rich Little Poor Girl: Sherri's Story Was Told in the Sissy Spacek Movie, 'A Private Matter'," www.veteranfeministsofamerica.org/legacy/Sherri%20Chessen.htm.

33 Edward Duffy, *The Effects of Changes in the State Abortion Laws*. Washington, DC: U.S. Department of Health, Education, and Welfare, Public Health Service, 1971.

34 "The Story of ALI," *American Legal Institute*, www.ali.org/about-ali/story-line/.

35 Markus D. Dubber, *An Introduction to the Model Penal Code*, 2nd ed. New York: Oxford University Press, 2015.

36 Roscoe Pound. "The Scope and Purpose of Sociological Jurisprudence." *Harvard Law Review* 25, no. 6 (1912): 489–516.

37 Thomas H. Barnard Jr, "An Analysis and Criticism of the Model Penal Code Provisions on the Law of Abortion," *Case Western Reserve Law Review* 18, no. 2 (1966): 540–564.

38 Thomas H. Barnard Jr, "An Analysis and Criticism of the Model Penal Code Provisions on the Law of Abortion," *Case Western Reserve Law Review* 18, no. 2 (1966): 540–564.

39 Kristin Luker, *Abortion and the Politics of Motherhood*. Berkeley, CA: University of California Press, 1984, 137.

40 Linda Greenhouse, *Becoming Justice Blackmun: Harry Blackmun's Supreme Court Journey*. New York: Times Books Henry Holt & Company, 2005, 80.

41 Randy Beck, "Self-Conscious Dicta: The Origins of Roe v. Wade's Trimester Framework," *American Journal of Legal History* 51 (2011): 505; "Pregnancy Week by Week," *Mayo Clinic*, www.mayoclinic.org/healthy-lifestyle/pregnancy-week-by-week/in-depth/prenatal-care/art-20045302; American College of Obstetricians and Gynecologists, "Facts Are Important: Gestational Development and Capacity for Pain," www.acog.org/advocacy/facts-are-important/gestational-development-capacity-for-pain.

42 Kaitlin Sullivan, "'Heartbeat Bills': Is There a Fetal Heartbeat at Six Weeks of Pregnancy?" *NBC News*, April 17, 2022, www.nbcnews.com/health/womens-health/heartbeat-bills-called-fetal-heartbeat-six-weeks-pregnancy-rcna24435.

43 James Robenalt, "January 22, 1973: The Day that Changed America," *The Washington Post*, January 22, 2022, www.washingtonpost.com/history/2022/01/22/january-22-1973-roe-vietnam-lbj/.

44 John Hart Ely, "The Wages of Crying Wolf: A Comment on *Roe v. Wade*," *The Yale Law Journal* 82, no. 5 (April 1973): 920–949, https://openyls.law.yale.edu/handle/20.500.13051/3571.

45 "The Silent Scream," *YouTube*, uploaded by CampaignLifeTV, www.youtube.com/watch?v=hstRrYsbffM.

46 Bernard Nathanson, *The Hand of God: A Journey from Death to Life by the Abortion Doctor Who Changed His Mind*. Washington, DC: Regnery Publishing, 1996, 140.

47   Ruth Marcus, "'Silent Scream': Loud Impact," *The Washington Post*, February 9, 1985, www.washingtonpost.com/archive/politics/1985/02/09/silent-scream-loud-impact/f8db85e8-d804-4b36-882f-4ae06303370b/.

48   National Abortion Federation, "NAF Violence and Disruption Statistics: Incidences of Violence and Disruption against Abortion Providers in the U.S. & Canada," www.prochoice.org/pubs_research/publications/downloads/about_abortion/violence_stats.pdf; Liam Stack, "A Brief History of Deadly Attacks on Abortion Providers," *The New York Times*, November 29, 2015, www.nytimes.com/interactive/2015/11/29/us/30abortion-clinic-violence.html.

49   Operation Rescue, "History," www.operationrescue.org/about-us/history/; Teach Democracy, "BRIA 16 3 c The Rescue Movement: Pushing the Limits of Free Speech," www.crf-usa.org/bill-of-rights-in-action/bria-16-3-c-the-rescue-movement-pushing-the-limits-of-free-speech.

50   Joseph M. Scheidler, *Closed: 99 Ways to Stop Abortion*. Washington, DC: Regnery Books, 1985.

51   "Randall Terry Interview," *The Forerunner*, September 1, 1998, www.forerunner.com/forerunner/X0471_Randall_Terry_Interv.

52   William Booth, "Doctor Killed during Abortion Protest," *The Washington Post*, March 11, 1993, www.washingtonpost.com/archive/politics/1993/03/11/doctor-killed-during-abortion-protest/e8adffc2-ba6f-459a-8c4b-4e547f7eb35b/.

53   Joan Finney, "Bill Limiting Access to Abortion Is Signed by Governor of Kansas," *New York Times*, April 24, 1992. ProQuest, www.nytimes.com/1992/04/24/us/bill-limiting-access-to-abortion-is-signed-by-governor-of-kansas.html.

54   Jennifer Donnally, "The Untold History Behind the 1991 Summer of Mercy," *Kansas History* 39, no. 4 (Winter 2016–2017): 245–261.

55   Susan Gluck Mezey, "Freedom of Access to Clinic Entrances Act of 1994 (1994)," *Freedom of Speech Center*, January 15, 2024, www.mtsu.edu/first-amendment/article/1080/freedom-of-access-to-clinic-entrances-act-of-1994#:~:text=the%20Associated%20Press)-,The%20Freedom%20of%20Access%20to%20Clinic%20Entrances%20Act%20of%201994,seeking%20abortions%20or%20other%20reproductive.

56   National Abortion Federation, "2022 Violence & Disruption Statistics," https://prochoice.org/wp-content/uploads/2022-VD-Report-FINAL.pdf.

57   Marcus Baram, "Randall Terry, Operation Rescue Founder, Says He's More Concerned About Obama's Reaction Than Tiller's Murder," *The Huffington Post* , May 25, 2011, www.huffpost.com/entry/randall-terry-operation-r_n_209531.

58   Centers for Disease Control, "Abortion Surveillance—Findings and Reports Abortion Surveillance 2021," www.cdc.gov/reproductivehealth/data_stats/abortion.htm.

59   "Abortions Later in Pregnancy," *KFF*, December 5, 2019, www.kff.org/womens-health-policy/fact-sheet/abortions-later-in-pregnancy/.; "Less Than 1% of Abortions Take Place in the Third Trimester—Here's Why People Get Them," *The Conversation*, May 17, 2022, https://theconversation.com/less-than-1-of-abortions-take-place-in-the-third-trimester-heres-why-people-get-them-182580.

60   American College of Obstetricians and Gynecologists, "ACOG Guide to Language and Abortion," www.acog.org/contact/media-center/abortion-language-guide.

61   "Less Than 1% of Abortions Take Place in the Third Trimester—Here's Why People Get Them," *The Conversation*, May 17, 2022, https://theconversation.com/less-than-1-of-abortions-take-place-in-the-third-trimester-heres-why-people-get-them-182580.

62   "Abortions Later in Pregnancy," *KFF*, December 5, 2019, www.kff.org/womens-health-policy/fact-sheet/abortions-later-in-pregnancy/.; "Less Than 1% of Abortions Take Place in the Third Trimester—Here's Why People Get Them," *The*

Conversation, May 17, 2022, https://theconversation.com/less-than-1-of-abortions-take-place-in-the-third-trimester-heres-why-people-get-them-182580.

63 "Less Than 1% of Abortions Take Place in the Third Trimester—Here's Why People Get Them," *The Conversation*, May 17, 2022, https://theconversation.com/less-than-1-of-abortions-take-place-in-the-third-trimester-heres-why-people-get-them-182580.

64 Transcript of the Second Oral Argument, *Roe v. Wade*, October 11, 1972, https://supreme.justia.com/cases/federal/us/410/113/.

65 Cynthia Gorney, "Gambling with Abortion: Why Both Sides Think They Have Everything to Lose," November 2004, https://harpers.org/archive/2004/11/gambling-with-abortion/.

66 Office of the Press Secretary, "Bill Clinton on Vetoing the Partial Birth Abortion Ban," *PBS News Hour*, April 10, 1996, www.pbs.org/newshour/politics/white_house-jan-june96-abortion_veto_04-10.

67 James Studnicki, "Late-Term Abortion and Medical Necessity: A Failure of Science," *Health Services Research and Managerial Epidemiology*, April 9, 2019; The American College of Obstetricians and Gynecologists, "Facts Are Important: Abortion Is Healthcare," www.acog.org/advocacy/facts-are-important/abortion-is-healthcare.

68 Janice Hopkins Tanne, "US Supreme Court Approves Ban on 'Partial Birth Abortion'," *British Medical Journal* 334, no. 7599 (April 28, 2007): 866–867; "The Supreme Court Revisits the Partial Birth Abortion Issue: *Gonzales v. Carhart* and *Gonzales v. Planned Parenthood*," November 1, 2006, www.pewresearch.org/religion/2006/11/01/the-supreme-court-revisits-the-partial-birth-abortion-issue/.

69 *Gonzales v. Carhart*, 550 U.S. 124, 2007.

70 Carey Goldberg, "Shots Assist in Aborting Fetuses: Lethal Injections Offer Legal Shield," *Boston Globe*, August 10, 2007; Lisa Haddad, Susan Yanow, Laurent Delli-Bovi, Kate Cosby and Tracy Weitz, "Changes in Abortion Provider Practices in Response to the Partial-Birth Abortion Ban Act of 2003," *Contraception* 79, no. (May 2009): 379–384.

71 Brittany Shammas, Aaron Steckelberg and Daniela Santamarina, "The Most Common Abortion Procedures and When They Occur," *The Washington Post*, June 24, 2022, www.washingtonpost.com/health/2022/06/21/abortion-procedures/.

72 "Abortions Later in Pregnancy," *KFF*, December 5, 2019, www.kff.org/womens-health-policy/fact-sheet/abortions-later-in-pregnancy/.; www.bpas.org/abortion-care/abortion-treatments/.

73 "Second Trimester Labor Induction Abortion," *Michigan Health and Human Services*, www.michigan.gov/mdhhs/adult-child-serv/informedconsent/michigans-informed-consent-for-abortion-law/procedures/second-trimester-labor-induction-abortion.

74 Rebecca J. Mercier, Mara Buchbinder and Amy Bryant, "TRAP Laws and the Invisible Labor of US Abortion Providers," *Critical Public Health* 26, no. 1: 77–87, www.tandfonline.com/doi/full/10.1080/09581596.2015.1077205; "Timeline of Attacks on Abortion: 2009–2021," *Planned Parenthood Action Fund*, www.plannedparenthoodaction.org/issues/abortion/abortion-central-history-reproductive-health-care-america/timeline-attacks-abortion.

75 *Whole Woman's Health v. Hellerstedt*, 579 U.S. 582, 2016.

76 Bonnie Jones, Sara Daniel and Lindsay Cloud, "State Law Approaches to Facility Regulation of Abortion and Other Office Interventions," *American Journal of Public Health* 108, no. 4 (April 2018): 486–492, www.ncbi.nlm.nih.gov/pmc/articles/PMC5844403/.

77 "Targeted Regulation of Abortion Providers," *The Guttmacher Institute*, August 31, 2023, www.guttmacher.org/state-policy/explore/targeted-regulation-abortion-providers.

78 "'We Have No Choice': A Story of the Texas Sonogram Law," *NPR Fresh Air*, January 22, 2013, www.npr.org/2013/01/22/169059701/we-have-no-choice-a-story-of-the-texas-sonogram-law.

79 Carolyn Jones, "'We Have No Choice': One Woman's Ordeal with Texas' New Sonogram LAW: The Painful Decision to Terminate a Pregnancy Is Now—Thanks to Texas' Harsh New Law—Just the Beginning of the Torment," *The Texas Observer*, March 15, 2012, www.texasobserver.org/we-have-no-choice-one-womans-ordeal-with-texas-new-sonogram-law/.

80 Erik Eckholm, "A Pawn in the Abortion Wars," *The New York Times*, February 25, 2012, www.nytimes.com/2012/02/26/sunday-review/ultrasound-a-pawn-in-the-abortion-wars.html.

81 Jen Russo, "Case and Commentary: Mandated Ultrasound Prior to Abortion," *American Medical Association Journal of Ethics, April 2014*, https://journalofethics.ama-assn.org/article/mandated-ultrasound-prior-abortion/2014-04.

82 "Whole Woman's Health v. Hellerstedt, 136 S. Ct. 22921 (2016)," *American Medical Association*, https://searchltf.ama-assn.org/case/documentDownload?uri=/unstructured/binary/case/Case-Summary_Whole-Womans-Health-v-Hellerstedt.pdf.

83 "Fourteenth Amendment—Due Process Clause—Undue Burden—Whole Woman's Health v. Hellerstedt," *Harvard Law Review* 130, no. 1 (November 2016): 397–406, https://harvardlawreview.org/print/vol-130/whole-womans-health-v-hellerstedt/.

84 Selena Simmons-Duffin and Carrie Feibel, "The Texas Abortion Ban Hinges on 'Fetal Heartbeat.' Doctors Call that Misleading," *NPR All Things Considered*, May 3, 2022, www.npr.org/sections/health-shots/2021/09/02/1033727679/fetal-heartbeat-isnt-a-medical-term-but-its-still-used-in-laws-on-abortion.

85 Jonathan F. Mitchell, "The Writ-of-Erasure Fallacy," *The Virginia Law Review* 101 (April 6, 2018): 933–1019, https://papers.ssrn.com/sol3/papers.cfm?abstract_id=3158038; www.wsj.com/articles/behind-texas-abortion-law-an-attorneys-unusual-enforcement-idea-11630762683.

86 Ian Millhiser, "The Staggering Implications of the Supreme Court's Texas Anti-Abortion Ruling," *Vox*, September 2, 2021, www.vox.com/22653779/supreme-court-abortion-texas-sb8-whole-womans-health-jackson-roe-wade.

87 Alan Braid, "Why I Violated Texas' Extreme Abortion Laws," *The Washington Post*, September 18, 2021, www.washingtonpost.com/opinions/2021/09/18/texas-abortion-provider-alan-braid/.

88 Ryan Autullo, "San Antonio Doctor Admits to Violating Texas' Controversial New Law on Abortions," *Austin American-Statesman*, September 19, 2021, www.statesman.com/story/news/2021/09/19/texas-abortion-law-san-antonio-doctor-alan-braid-violate-restrictions/8411084002/; "Lawsuits Filed against San Antonio Doctor Who Violated Texas Abortion Ban," *KVUE*, September 19, 2021, www.kvue.com/article/news/local/texas/san-antonio-doctor-pens-opinion-piece-on-why-he-violated-texas-abortion-ban/269-e59b7cbc-18f1-4783-b790-816a591fb7ca.

89 Amy Howe, "Supreme Court Leaves Texas Abortion Ban in Place," *SCOTUSblog*, September 2, 2021, www.scotusblog.com/2021/09/supreme-court-leaves-texas-abortion-ban-in-place/.

90 Casey Michelle Haining, Lousie Ann Keogh and Jullian Savulescu, "The Unethical Texas Heartbeat Law," *Prenatal Diagnosis* 42, no. 5 (May 2022): 535–541, www.ncbi.nlm.nih.gov/pmc/articles/PMC9320804/.

91 Amy Davidson Sorkin, "The Supreme Court Looks Ready to Overturn Roe v. Wade," *The New Yorker*, December 2, 2021, www.newyorker.com/news/daily-comment/the-supreme-court-looks-ready-to-overturn-roe; Lisa H. Harris, "Navigating Loss of Abortion Services—A Large Academic Medical Center Prepares for the Overturn of Roe v. Wade," *New England Journal of Medicine* 386 (June 2022): 2061–2064, www.nejm.org/doi/full/10.1056/NEJMp2206246.

92 Megan Messerly, "Abortion Laws by State: Where Abortions Are Illegal after *Roe v. Wade* Overturned," *Politico*, June 24, 2022, www.politico.com/news/2022/06/24/abortion-laws-by-state-roe-v-wade-00037695; Devan Cole and Tierney Sneed, "Where Abortion 'Trigger Laws' and Other Restrictions Stand after the Supreme Court Overturned Roe v. Wade," *CNN*, www.cnn.com/2022/06/27/politics/states-abortion-trigger-laws-roe-v-wade-supreme-court/index.html.

93 Jeffrey Rosen, "What Made Antonin Scalia Great," *The Atlantic*, February 15, 2016, www.theatlantic.com/politics/archive/2016/02/what-made-antonin-scalia-great/462837/.

94 Ron Elving, "What Happened with Merrick Garland in 2016 and Why It Matters Now," *NPR*, June 29, 2018, www.npr.org/2018/06/29/624467256/what-happened-with-merrick-garland-in-2016-and-why-it-matters-now.

95 Sarah McCammon, "What Justice Kennedy's Retirement Means for Abortion Rights," *NPR*, June 28, 2018, www.npr.org/2018/06/28/624319208/what-justice-kennedy-s-retirement-means-for-abortion-rights#:~:text=%22So%20we%20want%20Roe%20to,in%20Whole%20Woman's%20Health%20v.

96 Christine Hauser, "The Women Who Have Accused Brett Kavanaugh," *The New York Times*, September 26, 2018, www.nytimes.com/2018/09/26/us/politics/brett-kavanaugh-accusers-women.html#:~:text=Three%20women%20have%20publicly%20accused,latest%20allegation%20emerging%20on%20Wednesday.

97 Philip Ewing, "Granddaughter Presages Battle Royale: When Will New Justice Be Confirmed?" *NPR*, September 18, 2020, www.npr.org/sections/death-of-ruth-bader-ginsburg/2020/09/18/914643289/granddaughter-presages-battle-royale-when-will-new-justice-be-confirmed.

98 Chuck Schumer, "Schumer Floor Remarks on the Nomination of Judge Amy Coney Barrett to the United States Supreme Court," *Senate Democrats*, October, 26, 2020, www.democrats.senate.gov/newsroom/press-releases/schumer-floor-remarks-on-the-nomination-of-judge-amy-coney-barrett-to-the-united-states-supreme-court.

99 Michael Tarm, "Amy Coney Barrett, Supreme Court Nominee, Is Scalia's Heir," *AP*, September 26, 2020, https://apnews.com/article/election-2020-ruth-bader-ginsburg-chicago-us-supreme-court-courts-547b7de5b6ebabedee46b08b5bb37141.

100 John Hart Ely, "The Wages of Crying Wolf: A Comment on *Roe v. Wade*," *The Yale Law Journal* 82, no. 5 (April 1973): 920–949, https://openyls.law.yale.edu/handle/20.500.13051/3571.

101 Joan Biskupic, "The Inside Story of How John Roberts Failed to Save Abortion Rights," *CNN*, July 26, 2022, www.cnn.com/2022/07/26/politics/supreme-court-john-roberts-abortion-dobbs/index.html.

102 Sarah McCammon, "Two Months after the Dobbs Ruling, New Abortion Bans Are Taking Hold, *NPR*, August 23, 2022: 42, www.npr.org/2022/08/23/1118846811/two-months-after-the-dobbs-ruling-new-abortion-bans-are-taking-hold.

103 Lawrence O. Gostin, Sarah Wetter and Rebecca B. Reingold, "One Year After Dobbs—Vast Changes to the Abortion Legal Landscape," *JAMA Health Forum* 4, no 8. (2023), https://jamanetwork.com/journals/jama-health-forum/fullarticle/2808205.

104 Sean Murphy, "Oklahoma Governor Signs Nation's Strictest Abortion Law, Banning Procedure from 'Conception'," *PBS News Hour*, May 26, 2022, www.pbs.org/newshour/health/oklahoma-governor-signs-nations-strictest-abortion-law-banning-procedure-from-conception.

105 "State Constitutions and Abortion Rights," *Center for Reproductive Rights*, https://reproductiverights.org/state-constitutions-abortion-rights/.

106 "State Court Abortion Litigation Tracker," *Brennan Center*, January 11, 2024, www.brennancenter.org/our-work/research-reports/state-court-abortion-litigation-tracker; "After Roe Fell: Abortion Laws by State," *Center for Reproductive Rights*, https://reproductiverights.org/maps/abortion-laws-by-state/.

107 Anne M. Brendel and Rebecca Kennedy, "Implications of Abortion Laws for Fertility Services," *Goodwin*, www.goodwinlaw.com/en/insights/publications/2023/01/01_20-implications-of-abortion-laws-for-fertility-services.

108 "State Bans on Abortion Throughout Pregnancy," *Guttmacher Institute*, www.guttmacher.org/state-policy/explore/state-policies-later-abortions; and "State Legislation Tracker: Major Developments in Sexual & Reproductive Health," *Guttmacher Institute*, www.guttmacher.org/state-legislation-tracker.

109 Dahlia Lithwick, "Who Determines Kate Cox's Health Care," *Slate*, December 12, 2023. https://slate.com/news-and-politics/2023/12/kate-cox-nonviable-pregnancy-judicial-control-abortion-texas.html?utm_source=pocket_discover_health; Phillip Elliott, "That Texas Abortion Case Is Even Worse Than You Think,"*Time*,December 15,2023,https://time.com/6510970/abortion-texas-case/?utm_source=pocket_discover_self-improvement.

110 Center for Reproductive Rights, "State Constitutions and Abortion Rights," https://reproductiverights.org/maps/state-constitutions-and-abortion-rights/.

111 Guttmacher Institute, "Interactive Map: US Abortion Policies and Access After Roe," https://states.guttmacher.org/policies/colorado/abortion-policies.

112 Samuel L. Dickman, Kari White, David U. Himmelstein, Emily Lupez, Elizabeth Schrier and Steffie Woolhandler, "Rape-related Pregnancies in the 14 US States with Total Abortion Bans," *Internal Medicine* (January 24, 2024), https://jamanetwork.com/journals/jamainternalmedicine/fullarticle/2814274.

113 By: Louis Jacobson, "15 States with New or Impending Abortion Limits Have No Exceptions for Rape, Incest," *Poynter*, July 20, 2022, www.poynter.org/fact-checking/2022/post-roe-v-wade-state-bans-no-exceptions-rape-incest/.

114 Anne M. Brendel and Rebecca Kennedy, "Implications of Abortion Laws for Fertility Services," *Goodwin*, www.goodwinlaw.com/en/insights/publications/2023/01/01_20-implications-of-abortion-laws-for-fertility-services.

115 Gallup. "Where Do Americans Stand on Abortion?" Gallup, July 7, 2023. https://news.gallup.com/poll/321143/americans-stand-abortion.aspx.

116 "Legality of Abortion Demographic Tables," *Gallup*, https://news.gallup.com/poll/244097/legality-abortion-2018-demographic-tables.aspx.

117 *Union Pacific Railway Co. v. Botsford*, 141 U.S. 250, 1891.

118 *Olmstead v. United States*, 277 US 438, 1928.

119 *Skinner v. Oklahoma*, 316 U.S. 535, 1942.

120 *Loving v. Virginia*, 388 US 1, 1967.

121 *Roe v. Wade*, 410 U.S. 113, 1973.

122 *Planned Parenthood v. Casey*, 505 U.S. 833, 1992.

123 Rachel Jones et al., "Medication Abortion Now Accounts for More Than Half of All US Abortions," February 2022, www.guttmacher.org/article/2022/02/medication-abortion-now-accounts-more-half-all-us-abortions.

124 "Medication Abortion: Your Questions Answered," *Yale Medicine*, September 11, 2023, www.yalemedicine.org/news/medication-abortion-your-questions-answered; "Morning after Pill," *Mayo Clinic*, www.mayoclinic.org/tests-procedures/morning-after-pill/about/pac-20394730#:~:text=Plan%20B%20One%2DStep%20is,from%20implanting%20in%20the%20uterus.

125 Michel Martin and Selena Simmons-Duffin, "Federal Appeals Court Ruling Deals a Blow to Access to Abortion Pill Mifepristone," August 17, 2023, www.npr.org/2023/08/17/1194349562/federal-appeals-court-ruling-deals-a-blow-to-access-to-abortion-pill-mifepriston#:~:text=Art%20%26%20Design-,Federal%20appeals%20court%20ruling%20deals%20a%20blow%20to%20access%20to,status%20quo%20holds%20for%20now.

126 "'At Least 12 Million Babies' Since the First IVF Birth in 1978," *Focus on Reproduction*, June 28, 2023, www.focusonreproduction.eu/article/ESHRE-News-COP23_

adamson#:~:text=The%20ICMART%20preliminary%20data%20also,in%20
more%20than%2012%20million.

127 Tim Craig and Sabrina Malhi, "Shock, Anger, Confusion Grip Alabama after Court
Ruling on Embryos," *The Washington Post*, February 21, 2024, www.washing-
tonpost.com/nation/2024/02/20/alabama-supreme-court-ivf-embryos/; "Alabama
Families Face Uncertainty after Supreme Court IVF Ruling," *NBC News*, Feb-
ruary 28, 2024, www.nbcnews.com/now/video/alabama-families-face-uncer-
tainty-after-supreme-court-ivf-ruling-205156421882; Kim Chandler and Geoff
Mulvihill, "What's Next after the Alabama Ruling That Counts IVF Embryos as
Children?" *AP News*, February 22, 2024, https://apnews.com/article/alabama-
frozen-embryos-ivf-storage-questions-1adbc349e0f99851973a609e360c242c;
Joshua Sharfstein, "The Alabama Supreme Court's Ruling on Frozen Embryos,"
Johns Hopkins Bloomberg School of Public Health, February 27, 2024, https://
publichealth.jhu.edu/2024/the-alabama-supreme-courts-ruling-on-frozen-
embryos; "The Alabama Supreme Court's Ruling on Frozen Embryos," *Johns
Hopkins Bloomberg School of Public Health Public Health on Call*, February
27, 2024, https://johnshopkinssph.libsyn.com/bonus-the-alabama-supreme-
courts-ruling-on-frozen-embryos; Ari Shapiro, Linah Mohammad and Sarah
Handel, "After Alabama's Ruling, This Senator's Bill Aims to Protect National
Access to IVF," *NPR All Things Considered*, February 27, 2024, www.npr.
org/2024/02/27/1234158504/ivf-legislation-tammy-duckworth-alabama-
supreme-court; Michelle Boorstein, "Alabama Judge Says God Opposes IVF,
Religions Hold Varied Views," *The Washington Post*, February 28, 2024, www.
washingtonpost.com/nation/2024/02/28/alabama-ivf-embryos-religion-beliefs/;
Molly Hennessy-Fiske, "Red State Christian Women Are Rising Up, Speaking Out
to Defend IVF," *The Washington Post*, March 1, 2024, www.washingtonpost.com/
nation/2024/03/01/ivf-embryos-alabama-ruling-conservative-women/; Jessica
Glenza, "Alabama IVF Ruling Leaves Republicans Stuck Between Their Base and
The Broader Public," *The Guardian*, February 28, 2024, www.theguardian.com
/us-news/2024/feb/28/republicans-alabama-ivf-ruling.

128 Len Niehoff, "Unprecedented Precedent and Original Originalism: How the
Supreme Court's Decision in Dobbs Threatens Privacy and Free Speech Rights,"
American Bar Association, June 09, 2023, www.americanbar.org/groups/commu-
nications_law/publications/communications_lawyer/2023-summer/unprecedented-
precedent-and-original-originalism/.

129 Jay Edelson, "Post-Dobbs, Your Private Data Will Be Used Against You," *Bloomberg
Law*, September 22, 2022, https://news.bloomberglaw.com/us-law-week/post-dobbs-
your-private-data-will-be-used-against-you.

130 Grecia Rivera Rodriguez et al., "The Medical and Financial Burden of Illegal Abortion," *Cureus* 14, no. 10 (October 20, 2022), www.ncbi.nlm.nih.gov/pmc/articles/
PMC9675393/.

131 Willard Cates and Roger Rochat, "Illegal Abortions in the United States: 1972–
1974," *Family Planning Perspectives* (1976): 86–92.

132 Willard Cates and Roger Rochat, "Illegal Abortions in the United States: 1972–
1974," *Family Planning Perspectives* (1976): 86–92.

133 Jenna Jerman, Rachel Jones and Tsuyoshi Onda, "Characteristics of U.S. Abortion
Patients in 2014 and Changes Since 2008," May 2016, www.guttmacher.org/report/
characteristics-us-abortion-patients-2014.

134 Eugene Declercq, Ruby Barnard-Mayers, Laurie C. Zephyrin and Kay Johnson, "The
U.S. Maternal Health Divide: The Limited Maternal Health Services and Worse Out-
comes of States Proposing New Abortion Restrictions," *The Commonwealth Fund*,
December 14, 2022, www.commonwealthfund.org/publications/issue-briefs/2022/

dec/us-maternal-health-divide-limited-services-worse-outcomes#:~:text=In%20
addition%2C%20for%20every%20major,Hispanic%20people%20(Exhibit%205).
135　Rachel Benson Gold, "Lessons from Before Roe: Will Past be Prologue?" *Gutt-macher Policy Review* 6, no. 1 (March 1, 2003), www.guttmacher.org/gpr/2003/03/
lessons-roe-will-past-be-prologue.

References

"Abortions Later in Pregnancy." *KFF*, December 5, 2019. www.kff.org/womens-health-policy/fact-sheet/abortions-later-in-pregnancy/.

"Alabama Families Face Uncertainty after Supreme Court IVF Ruling." *NBC News*, Febru-ary 28, 2024. www.nbcnews.com/now/video/alabama-families-face-uncertainty-after-supreme-court-ivf-ruling-205156421882.

American College of Obstetricians and Gynecologists. "ACOG Guide to Language and Abortion." https://www.acog.org/contact/media-center/abortion-language-guide.

"The Alabama Supreme Court's Ruling on Frozen Embryos." *Johns Hopkins Bloomberg School of Public Health Public Health on Call*, February 27, 2024. https://johnshopkinssph.
libsyn.com/bonus-the-alabama-supreme-courts-ruling-on-frozen-embryos.

The American College of Obstetricians and Gynecologists. "Facts Are Important: Abortion Is Healthcare." www.acog.org/advocacy/facts-are-important/abortion-is-healthcare.

"'At Least 12 Million Babies' Since the First IVF Birth in 1978." *Focus on Reproduc-tion*, June 28, 2023. www.focusonreproduction.eu/article/ESHRE-News-COP23_
adamson#:~:text=The%20ICMART%20preliminary%20data%20also,in%20
more%20than%2012%20million.

Autullo, Ryan. "San Antonio Doctor Admits to Violating Texas' Controversial New Law on Abortions." *Austin American-Statesman*, September 19, 2021. www.statesman.
com/story/news/2021/09/19/texas-abortion-law-san-antonio-doctor-alan-braid-violate-restrictions/8411084002/.

Baram, Marcus. "Randall Terry, Operation Rescue Founder, Says He's More Concerned About Obama's Reaction Than Tiller's Murder." *The Huffington Post*, May 25, 2011.
www.huffpost.com/entry/randall-terry-operation-r_n_209531.

Barnard Jr., Thomas. "An Analysis and Criticism of the Model Penal Code Provisions on the Law of Abortion," *Case Western Reserve Law Review* 18, no. 2 (1966): 540–564.

Beck, Randy. "Self-Conscious Dicta: The Origins of Roe v. Wade's Trimester Frame-work." *American Journal of Legal History* 51 (2011): 505.

Biggs, M. Antonia, Heather Gould and Diana Greene Foster. "Understanding Why Women Seek Abortions in the U.S." *BMC Women's Health* 13, no. 1 (2013): 1–13.

Boorstein, Michelle. "Alabama Judge Says God Opposes IVF, Religions Hold Var-ied Views." *The Washington Post*, February 28, 2024. www.washingtonpost.com/
nation/2024/02/28/alabama-ivf-embryos-religion-beliefs/.

Booth, William. "Doctor Killed During Abortion Protest." *The Washington Post*,
March 11, 1993. www.washingtonpost.com/archive/politics/1993/03/11/doctor-killed-during-abortion-protest/e8adffc2-ba6f-459a-8c4b-4e547f7eb35b/.

Braid, Alan. "Why I Violated Texas' Extreme Abortion Laws." *The Washington Post*,
September 18, 2021. www.washingtonpost.com/opinions/2021/09/18/texas-abortion-provider-alan-braid/.

Brendel, Anne M. and Rebecca Kennedy. "Implications of Abortion Laws for Fertil-ity Services." *Goodwin*. www.goodwinlaw.com/en/insights/publications/2023/01/01
_20-implications-of-abortion-laws-for-fertility-services.

Brennan Center. "State Court Abortion Litigation Tracker." *Brennan Center*, January 11,
2024. https://www.brennancenter.org/our-work/research-reports/state-court-abortion-litigation-tracker.

Brown, Patrick. "Catholics are Just as Likely to Get an Abortion as Other U.S. Women. Why?" *American Magazine*, January 24, 2018. https://www.americamagazine.org/politics-society/2018/01/24/catholics-are-just-likely-get-abortion-other-us-women-why.

Biskupic, Joan. "The Inside Story of How John Roberts Failed to Save Abortion Rights." *CNN*, July 26, 2022. www.cnn.com/2022/07/26/politics/supreme-court-john-roberts-abortion-dobbs/index.html.

Cates, Willard, & Roger Rochat. "Illegal abortions in the United States: 1972–1974." *Family Planning Perspectives* (1976): 86–92.

Center for Reproductive Rights. "After Roe Fell: Abortion Laws by State." *Center for Reproductive Rights*. https://reproductiverights.org/maps/abortion-laws-by-state/.

Centers for Disease Control. "Abortion Surveillance—Findings and Reports Abortion Surveillance 2021." www.cdc.gov/reproductivehealth/data_stats/abortion.htm.

Chandler, Kim and Geoff Mulvihill. "What's Next after the Alabama Ruling That Counts IVF Embryos as Children?" *AP News*, February 22, 2024. https://apnews.com/article/alabama-frozen-embryos-ivf-storage-questions-1adbc349e0f99851973a609e360c242c.

Chessen, Sherri. "Rich Little Poor Girl: Sherri's Story Was Told in the Sissy Spacek Movie, 'A Private Matter'." www.veteranfeministsofamerica.org/legacy/Sherri%20Chessen.htm

Cohn, Nate. "Do Americans Support Abortion Rights? Depends on the State." *The New York Times*, May 4, 2022. www.nytimes.com/2022/05/04/upshot/polling-abortion-states.html.

Colburn, Don. "Abortion Rates Vary." *The Washington Post*, October 11, 1988. https://www.washingtonpost.com/archive/lifestyle/wellness/1988/10/11/abortion-rates-vary/4948caec-ec72-4028-b4d0-cd2e6873a73a/.

Cole, Devan and Tierney Sneed. "Where Abortion 'Trigger Laws' and Other Restrictions Stand after the Supreme Court Overturned Roe v. Wade." *CNN*. www.cnn.com/2022/06/27/politics/states-abortion-trigger-laws-roe-v-wade-supreme-court/index.html.

Craig, Tim and Sabrina Malhi. "Shock, Anger, Confusion Grip Alabama after Court Ruling on Embryos." *The Washington Post*, February 21, 2024. www.washingtonpost.com/nation/2024/02/20/alabama-supreme-court-ivf-embryos/.

Declercq, Eugune, Ruby Barnard-Mayers, Laurie C. Zephyrin and Kay Johnson. "The U.S. Maternal Health Divide: The Limited Maternal Health Services and Worse Outcomes of States Proposing New Abortion Restrictions." *The Commonwealth Fund*, December 14, 2022. www.commonwealthfund.org/publications/issue-briefs/2022/dec/us-maternal-health-divide-limited-services-worse-outcomes#:~:text=In%20addition%2C%20for%20every%20major,Hispanic%20people%20(Exhibit%205).

Dickman, Samuel, Kari White, David U. Himmelstein, Emily Lupez, Elizabeth Schrier, & Steffie Woolhandler. "Rape-related Pregnancies in the 14 US States with Total Abortion Bans." *Internal Medicine*, January 24, 2024. https://jamanetwork.com/journals/jamainternalmedicine/fullarticle/2814274.

Donnally, Jennifer. "The Untold History behind the 1991 Summer of Mercy." *Kansas History* 39, no. 4 (Winter 2016–2017): 245–261.

Dubber, Marcus. *An Introduction to the Model Penal Code*. Second Ed. New York: Oxford University Press, 2015.

Duffy, Edward. *The Effects of Changes in the State Abortion Laws*. Washington D.C.: U.S. Department of Health, Education, and Welfare, Public Health Service, 1971.

Eckholm, Erik. "A Pawn in the Abortion Wars." *The New York Times*, February 25, 2012. www.nytimes.com/2012/02/26/sunday-review/ultrasound-a-pawn-in-the-abortion-wars.html.

Edelson, Jay. "Post-Dobbs, Your Private Data Will Be Used Against You." *Bloomberg Law*, September 22, 2022. https://news.bloomberglaw.com/us-law-week/post-dobbs-your-private-data-will-be-used-against-you.

Eisenstadt v. Baird, 405 U.S. 438, 1972.

Ekland-Olson, Sheldon. *Who Lives, Who Dies, Who Decides?* 3rd ed., 135–142. New York: Routledge, 2018.

Elliott, Phillip. "That Texas Abortion Case Is Even Worse Than You Think." *Time*, December 15, 2023. https://time.com/6510970/abortion-texas-case/?utm_source= pocket_discover_self-improvement

Elving, Ron. "What Happened with Merrick Garland in 2016 and Why It Matters Now." *NPR*, June 29, 2018. www.npr.org/2018/06/29/624467256/what-happened-with-merrick-garland-in-2016-and-why-it-matters-now.

Ewing, Philip. "Granddaughter Presages Battle Royale: When Will New Justice Be Confirmed?" *NPR*, September 18, 2020. www.npr.org/sections/death-of-ruth-bader-ginsburg/2020/09/18/914643289/granddaughter-presages-battle-royale-when-will-new-justice-be-confirmed.

Finer, Lawrence B., Lori F. Frohwirth, Lindsay A. Dauphinee, Susheela Singh and Ann M. Moore. "Reasons U.S. Women Have Abortions: Quantitative and Qualitative Perspectives." September 2005. www.guttmacher.org/journals/psrh/2005/reasons-us-women-have-abortions-quantitative-and-qualitative-perspectives.

Finney, Joan. "Bill Limiting Access to Abortion is Signed by Governor of Kansas." *New York Times*, April 24, 1992. https://www.nytimes.com/1992/04/24/us/bill-limiting-access-to-abortion-is-signed-by-governor-of-kansas.html.

"Fourteenth Amendment—Due Process Clause—Undue Burden—Whole Woman's Health v. Hellerstedt." *Harvard Law Review* 130, no. 1 (November 2016): 397–406. https://harvardlawreview.org/print/vol-130/whole-womans-health-v-hellerstedt/.

Gallup. "Where Do Americans Stand on Abortion?" *Gallup*, July 7, 2023. https:// news.gallup.com/poll/321143/americans-stand-abortion.aspx.

Gladwell, Malcolm. "What the Co-Inventor of the Pill Didn't Know: Menstruation Can Endanger Women's Health." *The New Yorker*, March 5, 2000. https://www.newyorker. com/magazine/2000/03/13/john-rocks-error.

Glenza, Jessica. "Alabama IVF Ruling Leaves Republicans Stuck Between Their Base and the Broader Public." *The Guardian*, February 28, 2024. www.theguardian.com/ us-news/2024/feb/28/republicans-alabama-ivf-ruling.

Gold, Rachel Benson. "Lessons from Before Roe: Will Past Be Prologue?" *Guttmacher Policy Review* 6, no. 1 (March 1, 2003). www.guttmacher.org/gpr/2003/03/ lessons-roe-will-past-be-prologue.

Goldberg, Carey. "Shots Assist in Aborting Fetuses: Lethal Injections Offer Legal Shield." *Boston Globe*, August 10, 2007.

Gonzales v. Carhart, 550 U.S. 124, 2007.

Gorney, Cynthia. "Gambling with Abortion: Why Both Sides Think They Have Everything to Lose." November 2004. https://harpers.org/archive/2004/11/gambling-with-abortion/.

Gostin, Lawrence O., Sarah Wetter and Rebecca B. Reingold. "One Year After Dobbs—Vast Changes to the Abortion Legal Landscape." *JAMA Health Forum* 4, no 8 (2023). https://jamanetwork.com/journals/jama-health-forum/fullarticle/ 2808205.

Greenhouse, Linda. *Becoming Justice Blackmun: Harry Blackmun's Supreme Court Journey*, 80. New York: Times Books Henry Holt & Company, 2005.

Griswold v. Connecticut, 381 U.S. 479, 1965.

Guttmacher Institute. "Interactive Map: US Abortion Policies and Access After Roe." *Guttmacher Institute*. https://states.guttmacher.org/policies/colorado/abortion-policies.

Haddad, Lisa, Susan Yanow, Laurent Delli-Bovi, Kate Cosby and Tracy Weitz. "Changes in Abortion Provider Practices in Response to the Partial-Birth Abortion Ban Act of 2003." *Contraception* 79 (May 2009): 379–384.

Haining, Casey Michelle, Lousie Ann Keogh and Jullian Savulescu. "The Unethical Texas Heartbeat Law." *Prenatal Diagnosis* 42, no. 5 (May 2022): 535–541. www.ncbi. nlm.nih.gov/pmc/articles/PMC9320804/.

Harris, Lisa H. "Navigating Loss of Abortion Services—A Large Academic Medical Center Prepares for the Overturn of Roe v. Wade." *New England Journal of Medicine* 386 (June 2022): 2061–2064. www.nejm.org/doi/full/10.1056/NEJMp2206246.

Hart Ely, John. "The Wages of Crying Wolf: A Comment on Roe v. Wade." *The Yale Law Journal* 82, no. 5 (April 1973): 920–949. https://openyls.law.yale.edu/handle/20.500.13051/3571

Hartig, Hannah. "About Six-in-Ten Americans Say Abortion Should Be Legal in All or Most Cases." June, 13, 2022. www.pewresearch.org/fact-tank/2022/06/13/about-six-in-ten-americans-say-abortion-should-be-legal-in-all-or-most-cases-2/

Hauser, Christine. "The Women Who Have Accused Brett Kavanaugh." *The New York Times*, September 26, 2018. www.nytimes.com/2018/09/26/us/politics/brett-kavanaugh-accusers-women.html#:~:text=Three%20women%20have%20publicly%20accused,latest%20allegation%20emerging%20on%20Wednesday.

Hennessy-Fiske, Molly. "Red State Christian Women Are Rising Up, Speaking Out to Defend IVF." *The Washington Post*, March 1, 2024. www.washingtonpost.com/nation/2024/03/01/ivf-embryos-alabama-ruling-conservative-women/.

Howe, Amy. "Supreme Court Leaves Texas Abortion Ban in Place." *SCOTUSblog*, September 2, 2021. www.scotusblog.com/2021/09/supreme-court-leaves-texas-abortion-ban-in-place/.

Ingraham, Christopher. "Charted: The Religions that Make the Most Babies." *The Washington Post*, May 12, 2015. https://www.washingtonpost.com/news/wonk/wp/2015/05/12/charted-the-religions-that-make-the-most-babies/.

Jacobson, Louis. "15 States with New or Impending Abortion Limits Have No Exceptions for Rape, Incest." *Poynter*, July 20, 2022. https://www.poynter.org/fact-checking/2022/post-roe-v-wade-state-bans-no-exceptions-rape-incest/.

Jerman, Jenna, Rachel Jones and Tsuyoshi Onda. "Characteristics of U.S. Abortion Patients in 2014 and Changes Since 2008." May 2016. www.guttmacher.org/report/characteristics-us-abortion-patients-2014.

Joffe, Carole E., Tracy A. Weitz and Clare L. Stacey. "Uneasy Allies: Pro-choice Physicians, Feminist Health Activists and the Struggle for Abortion Rights." *Sociology of Health & Illness* 26, no. 6 (2004): 775–796.

Jones, Bonnie, Sara Daniel and Lindsay Cloud. "State Law Approaches to Facility Regulation of Abortion and Other Office Interventions." *American Journal of Public Health* 108, no. 4 (April 2018): 486–492. www.ncbi.nlm.nih.gov/pmc/articles/PMC5844403/

Jones, Carolyn. "'We Have No Choice': One Woman's Ordeal with Texas' New Sonogram LAW: The Painful Decision to Terminate a Pregnancy Is Now—Thanks to Texas' Harsh New Law—Just the Beginning of the Torment." *The Texas Observer*, March 15, 2012. www.texas-observer.org/we-have-no-choice-one-womans-ordeal-with-texas-new-sonogram-law/.

Jones, Rachel, Elizabeth Nash, Lauren Cross, Jesse Philbin and Marielle Kirstein. "Medication Abortion Now Accounts for More Than Half of All US Abortions." February 2022. www.guttmacher.org/article/2022/02/medication-abortion-now-accounts-more-half-all-us-abortions.

Jones, Rachel, Jesse Philbin, Marielle Kirstein, Elizabeth Nash and Kimberley Lufkin. "Long-Term Decline in US Abortions Reverses, Showing Rising Need for Abortion as Supreme Court Is Poised to Overturn Roe v. Wade."

January 1, 2022. www.guttmacher.org/article/2022/06/long-term-decline-us-abortions-reverses-showing-rising-need-abortion-supreme-court.

Kelly, Amita. "Fact Check: Was Planned Parenthood Started To 'Control' The Black Population?" *NPR*, August 14, 2015. https://www.npr.org/sections/itsallpolitics/2015/08/14/432080520/fact-check-was-planned-parenthood-started-to-control-the-black-population.

Kortsmit, Katherine, Antoinette T. Nguyen, Michele G. Mandel, Elizabeth Clark, Lisa M. Hollier, Jessica Rodenhizer and Maura K. Whiteman. "Abortion Surveillance—United States, 2020." *Surveillance Summaries* 71, no. 10 (November 25, 2022): 1–27. www.cdc.gov/mmwr/volumes/71/ss/ss7110a1.htm. www.guttmacher.org/article/2022/02/medication-abortion-now-accounts-more-half-all-us-abortions

"Lawsuits Filed against San Antonio Doctor Who Violated Texas Abortion Ban." *KVUE*, September 19, 2021. www.kvue.com/article/news/local/texas/san-antonio-doctor-pens-opinion-piece-on-why-he-violated-texas-abortion-ban/269-e59b7cbc-18f1-4783-b790-816a591fb7ca.

"Legality of Abortion Demographic Tables." *Gallup*. https://news.gallup.com/poll/244097/legality-abortion-2018-demographic-tables.aspx.

"Less than 1% of Abortions Take Place in the Third Trimester—Here's Why People Get Them." *The Conversation*, May 17, 2022. https://theconversation.com/less-than-1-of-abortions-take-place-in-the-third-trimester-heres-why-people-get-them-182580.

Lithwick, Dahlia. "Who Determines Kate Cox's Health Care." *Slate*, December 12, 2023. https://slate.com/news-and-politics/2023/12/kate-cox-nonviable-pregnancy-judicial-control-abortion-texas.html?utm_source=pocket_discover_health.

Loving v. Virginia, 388 US 1, 1967.

Luker, Kristin. *Abortion and the Politics of Motherhood*, 62–65. Berkeley, CA: University of California Press, 1984.

Marcus, Ruth. "'Silent Scream': Loud Impact." *The Washington Post*, February 9, 1985. www.washingtonpost.com/archive/politics/1985/02/09/silent-scream-loud-impact/f8db85e8-d804-4b36-882f-4ae06303370b/.

Martin, Michel and Selena Simmons-Duffin. "Federal Appeals Court Ruling Deals a Blow to Access to Abortion Pill Mifepristone." *NPR*, August 17, 2023. www.npr.org/2023/08/17/1194349562/federal-appeals-court-ruling-deals-a-blow-to-access-to-abortion-pill-mifepriston#:~:text=Art%20%26%20Design-,Federal%20appeals%20court%20ruling%20deals%20a%20blow%20to%20access%20to,status%20quo%20holds%20for%20now.

Mayo Clinic. "Pregnancy Week by Week." *Mayo Clinic*, https://www.mayoclinic.org/healthy-lifestyle/pregnancy-week-by-week/in-depth/prenatal-care/art-20045302.

McCammon, Sarah. "What Justice Kennedy's Retirement Means for Abortion Rights." *NPR*, June 28, 2018. www.npr.org/2018/06/28/624319208/what-justice-kennedy-s-retirement-means-for-abortion-rights#:~:text=%22So%20we%20want%20Roe%20to,in%20Whole%20Woman's%20Health%20v.

McCammon, Sarah. "Two Months after the Dobbs Ruling, New Abortion Bans Are Taking Hold, *NPR*, August 23, 2022: 42. www.npr.org/2022/08/23/1118846811/two-months-after-the-dobbs-ruling-new-abortion-bans-are-taking-hold.

"Medication Abortion: Your Questions Answered." *Yale Medicine*, September 11, 2023. www.yalemedicine.org/news/medication-abortion-your-questions-answered.

Mercier, Rebecca J., Mara Buchbinder and Amy Bryant. "TRAP Laws and the Invisible Labor of US Abortion Providers." *Critical Public Health* 26, no. 1 (2016): 77–87. www.tandfonline.com/doi/full/10.1080/09581596.2015.1077205

Messerly, Megan. "Abortion Laws by State: Where Abortions are Illegal after Roe v. Wade Overturned." *Politico*, June 24, 2022. www.politico.com/news/2022/06/24/abortion-laws-by-state-roe-v-wade-00037695.

Mezey, Susan Gluck. "Freedom of Access to Clinic Entrances Act of 1994 (1994)." *Freedom of Speech Center*, January 15, 2024. www.mtsu.edu/first-amendment/article/1080/freedom-of-access-to-clinic-entrances-act-of-1994#:~:text=the%20Associated%20Press)-,The%20Freedom%20of%20Access%20to%20Clinic%20Entrances%20Act%20of%201994,seeking%20abortions%20or%20other%20reproductive.

Michigan Health and Human Services. "Second Trimester Labor Induction Abortion." *Michigan Health and Human Services*. https://www.michigan.gov/mdhhs/adult-child-serv/informedconsent/michigans-informed-consent-for-abortion-law/procedures/second-trimester-labor-induction-abortion.

Millhiser, Ian. "The Staggering Implications of the Supreme Court's Texas Anti-Abortion Ruling." *Vox*, September 2, 2021. www.vox.com/22653779/supreme-court-abortion-texas-sb8-whole-womans-health-jackson-roe-wade.

Mitchell, Jonathan. "The Writ-of-Erasure Fallacy." *The Virginia Law Review* 101 (April 6, 2018): 933–1019. https://papers.ssrn.com/sol3/papers.cfm?abstract_id=3158038 ; www.wsj.com/articles/behind-texas-abortion-law-an-attorneys-unusual-enforcement-idea-11630762683.

Mohamed, Besheer, Hannah Hartig, Anna Schiller and Kelsey Beveridge. "America's Abortion Quandary." May 6, 2022, Pew Research Center. www.pewresearch.org/religion/2022/05/06/americas-abortion-quandary/.

"Morning after Pill." *Mayo Clinic*. www.mayoclinic.org/tests-procedures/morning-after-pill/about/pac-20394730#:~:text=Plan%20B%20One%2DStep%20is,from%20implanting%20in%20the%20uterus.

Murphy, Sean. "Oklahoma Governor Signs Nation's Strictest Abortion Law, Banning Procedure from 'Conception'." *PBS News Hour*, May 26, 2022. www.pbs.org/newshour/health/oklahoma-governor-signs-nations-strictest-abortion-law-banning-procedure-from-conception.

Nathanson, Bernard. *The Hand of God: A Journey from Death to Life by the Abortion Doctor Who Changed His Mind*, 140. Washington, DC: Regnery Publishing, 1996.

National Abortion Federation. "NAF Violence and Disruption Statistics: Incidences of Violence and Disruption against Abortion Providers in the U.S. & Canada." www.prochoice.org/pubs_research/publications/downloads/about_abortion/violence_stats.pdf.

Niehoff, Len. "Unprecedented Precedent and Original Originalism: How the Supreme Court's Decision in Dobbs Threatens Privacy and Free Speech Rights." *American Bar Association*, June 9, 2023. www.americanbar.org/groups/communications_law/publications/communications_lawyer/2023-summer/unprecedented-precedent-and-original-originalism/.

Office of the Press Secretary. "Bill Clinton on Vetoing the Partial Birth Abortion Ban." *I*, April 10, 1996. www.pbs.org/newshour/politics/white_house-jan-june96-abortion_veto_04-10.

Olmstead v. United States, 277 US 438, 1928.

Operation Rescue. "History." www.operationrescue.org/about-us/history/.

Pender, Caelyn. "'San Francisco Nine': The Case that Prompted California's Expansion of Abortion Laws." *KRON4*, July 24, 2022. https://www.kron4.com/news/san-francisco-nine-the-case-that-prompted-californias-expansion-of-abortion-laws/.

Planned Parenthood of Southeastern Pennsylvania v. Casey, 505 U.S. 833, 1991.

Pope Paul VI. "On the Regulation of Birth." *Humanae Vitae, Encyclical Letter*, July 25, 1968.

Potts, Malcom & Martha Campbell. "History of Contraception." *Gynecology and Obstetrics* 6, no. 8 (2002): 1–23.

Pound, Roscoe. "The Scope and Purpose of Sociological Jurisprudence." *Harvard Law Review* 25, no. 6 (1912): 489–516.

"Randall Terry Interview." *The Forerunner*, September 1, 1998. www.forerunner.com/forerunner/X0471_Randall_Terry_Interv

Reagan, Ronald. "Abortion and the Conscience of the Nation." *Human Life Review* 9, no. 2 (1983): 7–16.

Rivera Rodriguez, Grecia, Jean Tamayo Acosta, Ariel E Sosa Gomez, Rosymar E. Marcucci Rodriguez, Gissete A. Rodriguez Cintron and Marjorie Acosta. "The Medical and Financial Burden of Illegal Abortion", *Cureus* 14, no. 10 (October 20, 2022). www.ncbi.nlm.nih.gov/pmc/articles/PMC9675393/.

Robenalt, James. "January 22, 1973: The Day that Changed America." *The Washington Post*, January 22, 2022. www.washingtonpost.com/history/2022/01/22/january-22-1973-roe-vietnam-lbj/.

Rock, John. *The Time has Come: A Catholic Doctor's Proposals to End the Battle Over Birth Control*. New York: Avon Books, 1963.

Roe v. Wade. 410 U.S. 113, 1973.

Rosen, Jeffery. "What Made Antonin Scalia Great." *The Atlantic*, February 15, 2016. www.theatlantic.com/politics/archive/2016/02/what-made-antonin-scalia-great/462837/.

Russo, Jen. "Case and Commentary: Mandated Ultrasound Prior to Abortion." *American Medical Association Journal of Ethics*, April 2014. https://journalofethics.ama-assn.org/article/mandated-ultrasound-prior-abortion/2014-04.

Saad, Lydia. "Broader Support for Abortion Rights Continues Post-Dobbs." *Gallup*, June 14, 2023. https://news.gallup.com/poll/506759/broader-support-abortion-rights-continues-post-dobbs.aspx.

Scheidler, Joseph M. *Closed: 99 Ways to Stop Abortion*. Washington, DC: Regnery Books, 1985.

Shammas, Brittnay, Aaron Steckelberg & Daniela Santamarina. "The Most Common Abortion Procedures and When They Occur." *The Washington Post*, June 24, 2022. https://www.washingtonpost.com/health/2022/06/21/abortion-procedures/.

Shapiro, Ari Linah Mohammad and Sarah Handel. "After Alabama's Ruling, This Senator's Bill Aims to Protect National Access to IVF." *NPR All Things Considered*, February 27, 2024. www.npr.org/2024/02/27/1234158504/ivf-legislation-tammy-duckworth-alabama-supreme-court.

Sharfstein, Joshua. "The Alabama Supreme Court's Ruling on Frozen Embryos." *Johns Hopkins Bloomberg School of Public Health*, February 27, 2024. https://publichealth.jhu.edu/2024/the-alabama-supreme-courts-ruling-on-frozen-embryos.

Shumer, Chuck. "Schumer Floor Remarks on the Nomination of Judge Amy Coney Barrett to the United States Supreme Court." *Senate Democrats*, October, 26, 2020. www.democrats.senate.gov/newsroom/press-releases/schumer-floor-remarks-on-the-nomination-of-judge-amy-coney-barrett-to-the-united-states-supreme-court.

"The Silent Scream." *YouTube*. Uploaded by CampaignLifeTV. www.youtube.com/watch?v=hstRrYsbffM.

Simmons-Duffin, Selena and Carrie Feibel. "The Texas Abortion Ban Hinges on 'Fetal Heartbeat.' Doctors Call that Misleading." *NPR All Things Considered*, May 3, 2022. www.npr.org/sections/health-shots/2021/09/02/1033727679/fetal-heartbeat-isnt-a-medical-term-but-its-still-used-in-laws-on-abortion.

Skinner v. Oklahoma, 316 U.S. 535, 1942.

Sorkin, Amy Davidson. "The Supreme Court Looks Ready to Overturn Roe v. Wade." *The New Yorker*, December 2, 2021. www.newyorker.com/news/daily-comment/the-supreme-court-looks-ready-to-overturn-roe.

Stack, Liam. "A Brief History of Deadly Attacks on Abortion Providers." *The New York Times*, November 29, 2015. www.nytimes.com/interactive/2015/11/29/us/30abortion-clinic-violence.html.

"State Bans on Abortion Throughout Pregnancy." *Guttmacher Institute*. www.guttmacher.org/state-policy/explore/state-policies-later-abortions.

"State Constitutions and Abortion Rights." *Center for Reproductive Rights.* https://repro-ductiverights.org/state-constitutions-abortion-rights/.

"State Legislation Tracker: Major Developments in Sexual & Reproductive Health." *Guttmacher Institute.* www.guttmacher.org/state-legislation-tracker. https://news.gal-lup.com/poll/321143/americans-stand-abortion.aspx.

Stenberg v. Carhart, 530 U.S. 914, 2000.

Stone, Abraham. "Social and Legal Status of Contraception, The-Part I." *North Carolina Law Review* 22, no. 3 (1944): 212.

Stone, Lyman. "America's Growing Religious-Secular Fertility Divide." *Institute for Family Studies*, August 8, 2022. https://ifstudies.org/blog/americas-growing-religious-secular-fertility-divide.

Studnicki, James. "Late-Term Abortion and Medical Necessity: A Failure of Science." *Health Services Research and Managerial Epidemiology*, April 9, 2019.

Sullivan, Kaitlin. "'Heartbeat bills': Is There a Fetal Heartbeat at Six Weeks of Pregnancy?" *NBC News*, April 17, 2022. https://www.nbcnews.com/health/womens-health/heartbeat-bills-called-fetal-heartbeat-six-weeks-pregnancy-rcna24435.

"The Story of ALI." *American Legal Institute.* https://www.ali.org/about-ali/story-line/.

"The Supreme Court Revisits the Partial Birth Abortion Issue: Gonzales v. Carhart and Gonzales v. Planned Parenthood." November 1, 2006. www.pewresearch.org/religion/2006/11/01/the-supreme-court-revisits-the-partial-birth-abortion-issue/.

Tanne, Janice Hopkins. "US Supreme Court Approves Ban on 'Partial Birth Abortion'." *British Medical Journal* 334, no. 7599 (April 28, 2007): 866–867.

"Targeted Regulation of Abortion Providers." *The Guttmacher Institute*, August 31, 2023. www.guttmacher.org/state-policy/explore/targeted-regulation-abortion-providers.

Tarm, Michael. "Amy Coney Barrett, Supreme Court Nominee, Is Scalia's Heir." *AP*, September 26, 2020. https://apnews.com/article/election-2020-ruth-bader-ginsburg-chicago-us-supreme-court-courts-547b7de5b6ebabedee46b08b5bb37141.

Teach Democracy. "BRIA 16 3 c the Rescue Movement: Pushing the Limits of Free Speech." www.crf-usa.org/bill-of-rights-in-action/bria-16-3-c-the-rescue-movement-pushing-the-limits-of-free-speech.

"Timeline of Attacks on Abortion: 2009–2021." *Planned Parenthood Action Fund.* www.plannedparenthoodaction.org/issues/abortion/abortion-central-history-reproductive-health-care-america/timeline-attacks-abortion.

Transcript of the Second Oral Argument, *Roe v. Wade*, October 11, 1972. https://supreme.justia.com/cases/federal/us/410/113/.

Union Pacific Railway Co. v. Botsford, 141 U.S. 250, 1891.

Webster v. Reproductive Health Services, 492 U.S. 490, 1989.

"'We Have No Choice': A Story of the Texas Sonogram Law." *NPR Fresh Air*, January 22, 2013. www.npr.org/2013/01/22/169059701/we-have-no-choice-a-story-of-the-texas-sonogram-law.

Whole Woman's Health v.Hellerstedt, 579 U.S. 582, 2016.

"Whole Woman's Health v. Hellerstedt, 136 S. Ct. 22921 (2016)." *American Medical Association.* https://searchltf.ama-assn.org/case/documentDownload?uri=/unstructured/binary/case/Case-Summary_Whole-Womans-Health-v-Hellerstedt.pdf.

Zeigler, Mary. "Eugenic Feminism: Mental Hygiene, the Women's Movement, and the Campaign for Eugenic Legal Reform, 1900–1935." *Harvard Journal of Law and Gender* 31 (2008): 211.

Index

For Product Safety Concerns and Information please contact our EU
representative GPSR@taylorandfrancis.com
Taylor & Francis Verlag GmbH, Kaufingerstraße 24, 80331 München, Germany

www.ingramcontent.com/pod-product-compliance
Lightning Source LLC
Chambersburg PA
CBHW050719280326
41926CB00088B/3329

9 781032 554228